WE ARE ALL GOD'S POEMS

Edited by Shann Ray, Cinnamon Kills First, Keya Mitra Lloyd, José Hernandez, Patricia Valdés, and Charles Finn

WE ARE ALL GOD'S POEMS

Copyright © 2024 Shann Ray, Cinnamon Kills First, Keya Mitra Lloyd, José Hernandez, Patricia Valdés, and Charles Finn. All poems in this book are copyrighted to the poets who graciously supplied a poem for this anthology.

All Rights Reserved.

Published by Unsolicited Press.

Printed in the United States of America.

First Edition.

No part of this book may be used or reproduced in any manner whatsoever without written permission except in the case of brief quotations embodied in critical articles or reviews. People, places, and notions in these poems are from the author's imagination; any resemblance to real persons or events is purely coincidental.

Gratitude to the enigmatic source for the grant provided to make this project a reality.

Attention schools and businesses: for discounted copies on large orders, please contact the publisher directly.

For information contact:
Unsolicited Press
Portland, Oregon
www.unsolicitedpress.com
orders@unsolicitedpress.com
619-354-8005

Cover Design: Kathryn Gerhadt
Editors: Shann Ray, Cinnamon Kills First, Keya Mitra Lloyd, José Hernandez, Patricia Valdés, and Charles Finn
Managing Editor: Summer Stewart
ISBN: 978-1-963115-22-2

A WORD BEFORE

IN LIGHT of the loneliness and unsettling experienced in the wake of the pandemic and the trauma so common to the embattlements of political life, work life, and family life, six poets got together to make a response grounded in hope and love. As we gathered, we felt the desolation of living in what might be called an age of enragement, victimhood, and human rights abuses, and so we decided to create a poetry anthology that might quietly speak to the multivalent beauty of humanity.

When we started this project, we found ourselves unmoored by the deepest fractures, so painful and inherent in the history, present, and future of our national and international communities. We began to speak of love, and how poetry might respond to the depth of sorrow we felt. We came upon the idea that people aren't only God's children as is so often said, but each of us is one of God's poems, however we may experience God or seek to define or encompass God.

Yet there is an ancient and humbling wisdom that states if we think we understand God, it isn't God.

Throughout humanity the notion of God is elusive, from the unnamable God of so many traditions, to Ma'heo of the Cheyenne nation, to the Anima Christi represented by the hanging crucifix in Barcelona's La Sagrada Familia, to the essence of a spirit of good in the lived world, to the existential courage of facing the world through an atheistic lens... we recognize no one has the right to define God, just as no one has the right to deny the generosity and grace found in the gift of a song, a kind word, or a loving touch.

The editors of this book of collected poems are Shann Ray, Cinnamon Kills First, Keya Mitra Lloyd, Patricia Valdés, José Hernandez, and Charles Finn. We sought poems that might embody our mutual sisterhood, brotherhood, and unity across racial, gender, socioeconomic, sexual orientation, cultural, and all other intersectionality.

We committed ourselves to help shape this volume of poems and as the poems came in from places as far as Ireland and Qatar, and as near as our hometowns, we found the strength of the poems in this volume stunning, compassionate, and united in a common desire for shared meaning. The poems that arrived made us laugh and cry, drew us deeper into a sense of sacredness, and brought us closer to each other.

In imagining what this book might become we found inspiration in the feminist warrior poet Audre Lorde, who was born in Harlem in 1934 and died in St. Croix, U.S. Virgin Islands, in 1992. She lived as a freedom fighter seeking to serve the deepest needs of people to create a more just world. Her critique of dominant patriarchy resounds: "The master's tools will never dismantle the master's house. They may allow us to temporarily beat him at his own game, but they will never enable us to bring about genuine change." In the truest sense of the word, Lorde *led* people and nations into greater love and freedom. With her life and poetry, she showed how the legitimate power associated with serving the highest priority needs of others can help heal the heart of the peoples of the world, especially the least respected.

Lorde championed those Cornel West identified as the wretched of the earth, a moniker imbued with clarion transparency by Frantz Fanon: the least of these being those we are unified with, indebted to, and with whom we share humility, *humu*s, the earth that bears the imprint of our feet and the hope of a more humane existence. Ill dominant culture tendencies wound the world, leaving in their wake power abuses of all forms, severe lack of emotional intelligence, hyper-rational lack of love, a history of genocide, and the aftereffects of the generational narcissistic injury so prevalent in America today. Lorde, a self-described "black, lesbian, mother, warrior, womanist, poet" who lived and created through directly challenging intersectional injustice wrote in *The Black Unicorn*:

> and when we speak we are afraid
>
> our words will not be heard
>
> nor welcomed
>
> but when we are silent
>
> we are still afraid
>
> So it is better to speak
>
> remembering
>
> we were never meant to survive

Audre Lorde wielded poetry on the threshing floor of injustice, harvesting love.

Like Audre, we offer these poems to embody hope and give hope.

Our wish as you encounter the poets included in this anthology is that they also bring a small sense of peace. Four different generations are represented here, State Poet Laureates alongside Stegner fellows, beginners alongside award winners. Following each poem is a statement from the poet regarding influence (marked with a ◊) as well as a biography. May these voices come into your life as they have into ours, enriching and awakening, descending like fresh rain, resounding with a familiar and beautiful music, shining light into darkness.

The notion of an abiding intimacy, informing these poems and championed by bell hooks, Viktor Frankl and many others, suggests something we find to be a longing in our collective humanity, alongside the difficulties, entanglements, and complexities that attend our lives. The experience of love, like the experience of a smile, achieves almost immediate affirmation of the existence of a transcendent essence in the world. Now, as the world continues in a kind of wrestling with the thick darkness of fascism alongside how we encounter the gravity of our own lives, poetry becomes more and more vital. In the shadow of the Holocaust, Viktor Frankl had the audacity to say this: "The salvation of [humanity] is through love and in love. I understood how a [person] who has nothing left in this world still may know bliss, be it only for a brief moment, in the contemplation of [the] beloved." Frankl also echoed the basic intimacy of our biology when he said:

> Consider the eye. The eye, too, is self-transcendent in a way. The moment it perceives something of itself, its function—to perceive the surrounding world visually—has deteriorated. If it is afflicted with a cataract, it may 'perceive' its own cataract as a cloud; and if it is suffering from glaucoma, it might 'see' its own glaucoma as a rainbow halo around lights. Normally, however, the eye doesn't see anything of itself.
>
> To be human is to strive for something outside of oneself. I use the term "self-transcendence" to describe this quality behind the will to meaning, the grasping for something or someone outside oneself. Like the eye, we are made to turn outward toward another human being to whom we can love and give ourselves.
>
> Only in such a way do people demonstrate themselves to be truly human.

> Only when in service of another does a person truly know his or her humanity.

Like Viktor Frankl, Audre Lorde lived in accord with revolutionaries of freedom and those who abandon themselves to love everywhere. She addressed injustices of racism, sexism, classism, heterosexism, and homophobia. Her voice resounds today, the song of a poet who leads us to greater wisdom, health, autonomy, connection, freedom, and communion. Her art unites us in the warm home of her essential understanding and sends us back into the world prepared not only to see more clearly but to love more deeply, not only to challenge but to bring healing. "Pain is important," she said, "how we evade it, how we succumb to it, how we deal with it, how we transcend it... Revolution is not a one-time event."

In *We Are All God's Poems*, we are grateful to the poets for giving us the strength to go forward, arm in arm with you, toward hope.

In appreciation and with fortitude,
Shann, with Cinnamon, Keya, José, Patricia, and Charles

WE ARE ALL GOD'S POEMS

WE ARE ALL GOD'S POEMS
Kelli Russell Agodon

All morning barnacles have split
like seaside atoms, and above—a moonlight
of gulls circling as if they will unlock

the shore with their patterns. My shadow leans
into the waves and I think of the time a stranger
pulled me from an undertow when currents

flipped me upside-down. A misunderstanding
of ocean where I tumbled to the bottom of the sea.
Underwater, sunlight is the open door

one must follow knowing when we arrive
our mouths will open to air and we will smell
the scent of fireweed miles away, the figs

our grandfather grew in another country
even as we waltzed in love with pears
and starlight nowhere near his childhood home.

Tell me, when you look into the eyes of a stranger,
what do you see? Rainfall or sunshine? An infant
who struggled to walk or heartbeats beneath

a ribcage? I want to listen to the language
of eyelashes, to find the possibilities in seaglass
and blessings we pass like sand dollars,

acknowledging their beauty briefly as we continue
tromping over an unkempt beach. Below a concerto
of whitecaps, there are miracles

in paying attention, in a body diving under
to rescue another, a small child like an electron
of the sea, how our reflections appeared

in the slack tide, faith reawakened, to trust
in each other, one hand reaching into a mirror,
the other holding on for her life.

◊*Like the Blanche DuBois quote from A Streetcar Named Desire, "I have always depended on the kindness of strangers." In fact, there have been several times I have avoided harm because someone was paying attention for my well-being. This poem reflects my thankfulness to the humans who in a moment, make a difference in another's life and remind me how we (and our actions) are all connected.*

Kelli Russell Agodon's fourth collection of poems is *Dialogues with Rising Tides* (Copper Canyon Press, 2021). She is the cofounder of Two Sylvias Press and the Co-Director of Poets on the Coast: A Weekend Retreat for Women. You can write to her directly at kelli@agodon.com or visit her website: www.agodon.com

WE ARE ALL GOD'S POEMS
Sandra Alcosser

~

Sometimes I live in the Holy
Land of pretend where no
Animal is eaten -- only watched over
Where mourning cloaks
Shiver on willows
Blue bees sleep in tiny motels waiting
For love to find them to waken
Be offered a sweetmeat of pollen
Where a bison calf might fall -- eyes open
Kicking and dancing its first moments
Like one desiring not to be eaten
Where grasses beg the calf's leavings
From which will sprout kingdoms
of insects and new seeds

◊*I was fortunate to have as a friend and teacher William Kittredge who wrote this bit of sanity: We must define a story which encourages us to make use of the place where we live without killing it, and we must understand that the living world cannot be replicated. There will never be another setup like the one in which we have thrived. Ruin it and we will have lost ourselves, and that is craziness.*

Sandra Alcosser's *A Fish to Feed All Hunger* and *Except by Nature* received highest honors from the National Poetry Series, Academy of American Poets and AWP Award Series. She's received three National Endowment for the Arts fellowships, served as Montana's poet laureate, directs SDSU's MFA each fall and is the Editor of *Poetry International*.

WE ARE ALL GOD'S POEMS
Ariana Alexis

I saw a sparrow soaring
beneath a swift cloud.

The body lifted
and fell in the wind
and as I watched, another sparrow
rose up to join her.
Their flight was entwined
in a spiral of air
before they broke apart

while she kept soaring
and he fell back
to follow her.

They disappeared
and I didn't see anything
for a long time.

Then they came back to me
this time beside each other
flying down
and down
beneath the distant frame

of Scissortail Park
before rising again
accompanied by a dozen more.

Together
they flew out of sight

and I knew
they were for me.

◊*I noticed the sparrows on an April day and they've remained in memory since. They seemed as if they were sent to me as a reminder of the inestimable peace of God amidst despair.*

Ariana Alexis is a senior at Oklahoma City University studying music theatre and vocal performance. She plans to move to New York after graduation to be with her sister Natalya and pursue a career in artistry and music. She has been drawn to poetry and classic literature and has been influenced by writers such as Gerard Manly Hopkins, Emily Dickinson, and Melanie Rae Thon.

WE ARE ALL GOD'S POEMS
Bella Alexis

Dear God, thank you

for your everlasting kindness,
mercy and light.

Do you remember how my grandfather
told me before he died, strength is in the
quietness and stillness?

I remember too how I held his hand.
I was eight years old, sunlight in the open window,
and from the sky the smell of autumn.

You're a miracle, he said. This before
the pain he suffered until death.
I won't forget, he was a man of immense joy.
His wife and daughter, his granddaughters, his mother
thank God for him for he did not harm them and saw them rise.

In the darkness, immense silence.

I am a portfolio of work dedicated
to unity and fracture. I am the painted red hand,
erasure, my mouth sewn shut
by the femicide that is America.
I won't forget my grandfather and the men
who heal me. They walk with me
and we heal her together, this nation of ill will
and murder. Listen! We cannot eat
hatred any longer. We must learn
to love and be loved. We must encounter

the women of this broken earth
who walk who shapeshift in bare feet as Romeo and Juliet
rising to give themselves like van Gogh's black crows
gave the sower a golden robe she wears forever.

I heard him whisper on that final day
the greatest work of art is to love someone.

God, thank you for giving me ears to hear.

◊*In writing this poem I thought of the art I've viewed, embodied, and composed. I am primarily a painter so the opportunity to engage through line, rhythm, and sound became a practice of narrative painting.*

Bella Alexis is a first-year student of art and psychology at Pepperdine University. She was a Youth Justice Advocate for Embers International in Mumbai, India, and she seeks to view people and the world through a lens of beauty and truth.

WE ARE ALL GOD'S POEMS
AMINAH

I met lost innocence in a dream,
While crashing into a foreign stream
Distant, but familiar to me.

On the riverbank,
Tiny clothes were hanging,
Clothes found on school children playing.

White linen, blue floral stitching,
Stripped by thieves with ill intentions,
Children's toys replaced with ammunition.

I met lost innocence in a dream,
While crashing into another stream
Distant, but familiar to me.

Tiny feet that crossed a wide ravine,
Torn from their mothers, savagely,
Spirits, forever, marked by tragedy.

I met lost innocence in a dream,
While crossing a domestic stream
Close, and so familiar to me.

Stolen children removed from peace,
Tiny braids snipped, and bodies beat.
I can still hear their screams.

We are all God's children,
Yet we enlist the innocent
to settle adult conflict.

We are all God's poems,
Yet the words from my soul
struggle to find a home.

◊*I was inspired to write this poem after waking up from a mysterious dream in which I found myself crashing into a river in another country. I found children's school uniforms on the bank of the river, and other parts of my dream indicated that I was seeing the abandoned school clothes of child soldiers in the Congo. I wanted this poem to express the deep pain that I felt for their stolen innocence, along with the other tragedies we witness against children in the migrant camps at the U.S./Mexico Border, and the Indigenous children lost in Catholic boarding schools during the Assimilation period.*

Aminah is a Lumbee and Black advocate from Pembroke, NC. She studied Biology at East Carolina University, and Physiology & Biophysics with a concentration in Integrative Medicine. She is an athlete, artist, researcher, advocate for MMIP, and finding common humanity between marginalized communities and allies.

WE ARE ALL GOD'S POEMS
Chris Anderson

Baptizing Rosa Guadalupe

The little girl in a gauzy white dress
and beaded tiara. Her father in a pressed white shirt
and jeans, his dark face solemn and intent
as he tries to understand the words. I feel so clumsy.

So distant. But then I cup the water
in my hand, and I pour it on his daughter's head,
on her jet-black hair, and I look up at him,
and he looks up at me, and for a moment we meet.

We know. The way sometimes before we fall
asleep there is an image in our minds,
or a fragrance, or a melody we don't remember
when we wake up, the beginning of a story

we only understand at just the moment
we finally let go.

◊ *This poem was the gift of two experiences: the experience of baptizing this little girl, and the gulf I felt, and then the connection; and the experience of a dream and the lingering coherence of a dream, just out of reach. It was when I realized that these two experiences were related, that there was something hidden in the space between them, that the poem fell into place. It was a gift!*

Chris Anderson is a Catholic deacon, a recently retired professor of English at Oregon State University, and a poet and essayist. His most recent book of poems is *You Never Know*, published by Stephen F. Austin State University Press in 2018.

WE ARE ALL GOD'S POEMS…
DAVID AXELROD

or their traces, falling onto your wrists

the way rain fell on ours last June,

picking the sweetest things

that day—scallions and snow peas

we shared with grandchildren,

whose absence forced us to pretend,

in these mountains across a country

they don't yet know they're citizens of

by no choice of their own. The rain fell

the way music or thawing forest

fills the air, the porous brink of the present

weighting everything

with its denser gravity, unseen

but felt—our lord of similitudes, sometimes

yes, sometimes nothing,

and so abashed he fled his world

and people, who we surely are,

hammered metal, knotted star. At the verge

of twilight, in the eleventh month of pandemic,

to whom do we offer these muttered

blessings if not for grandchildren, our faith

in what remains unseen, the pulse inside

of words we still hold dear, felt far away.

◊*In the wake of the January 6 Insurrection, I turned to Yeats's "Meditations in Time of Civil War," not so much for comfort (he doesn't really offer any), but for a reminder of the consequences of being fed fantasies, of placing "More substance in our enmities / Than our love." It wasn't, however, the escalating despair of "The Stare's Nest by My Window," that was most clarifying. Rather, it was in the unlikely stuffiness of "Ancestral Houses" that I found the affirmation of faith I sought, of a living world undistorted by madness. "Life," Yeats wrote, "overflows without ambitious pain," and "out of life's own self-delight had sprung / The abounding glittering jet." As my poem "or their traces, falling onto your wrists" began to emerge, soldiers patrolled my grandchildren's street in Washington, D.C. As they live in an historically black neighborhood and are themselves of mixed background, I feared for them in that city awash in the moment with racist menace, antipathy, and violence, all the consequence of lies. Poems are poor protection for the vulnerable, I know, but life survives in the freedom to praise.*

David Axelrod is the author of eight collections of poetry, most recently, *The Open Hand*, and two collections of nonfiction, including *The Eclipse I Call Father: Essays on Absence*. He directs the low residency MFA at Eastern Oregon University and edits *basalt: a journal of fine & literary arts*.

WE ARE ALL GOD'S POEMS
G D Barnes

What – under shades of sun & dark,
under shadow of wind-blurred leaf,
under clouds that bump & push
like crowds leaving the station –
are we to do?

How shape our days as they pass through us?

Why love when love ends in loss?
Why love in a world broken
like a hammered vase?

Because the rose asks us.
Because light each day calls us from sleep.

Because light always, when looked at squarely
eyes wide attending
stuns with wonder
whatever the trash & heartbreak
heaped in our streets.

Because clouds write our mysteries.
'Because love, like light, unhides the hidden.
Because love heals like a mother's hand
on the child's angry brow.

◊*I puzzled on how an obdurate agnostic, afflicted with a chronic mysticism, might best fit a poem to this title. The first stanza's essential question seemed to write itself. A momentum of questions followed, followed by a momentum of tentative answers. Vase suggested rose (in a line that feels like Rilke whispered in my ear). The paradox of our simultaneous awe at the miracle of presence and agony at our often self-inflicted disasters, needs voices. I tried to make one.*

G D Barnes has been writing poetry for over 50 years. He worked with Carolyn Forché at Michigan State, and Albert Goldbarth & A. R. Ammons at Cornell University in the 70's. He was a PEW Fellowship of the Arts Finalist in Poetry in 2001, the same year for which he was awarded "Poem of the Year" by the Philadelphia City Paper. He has served as a professor at Peirce College in Philadelphia and as a lawyer. He lives in Redwood City CA, Philadelphia PA & Lisbon Portugal with his cherished wife, Ruth Shaber.

WE ARE ALL GOD'S POEMS
Carol Barrett

We begin this life, dripping
placental blood, are revived
and revised many times over,
washed clean of whatever
mess we have gotten into,
our verbs more deliberate,
faces more contrite. As our voices
tumble into litanies of outrage
or repentance, sonnets of sorrow
or humility, we learn to edit
consciousness, to become
glad seekers of truth, conjunctions
of neighborly love, to abide in a holy
place, despite raucous
temptations to the contrary.

A public health nurse, my sister
delivered babies in rural Oregon,
shanties built on riverbanks
flowing in earnest. She partook
of a ritual of grateful nourishment:
placenta baked in a deep dish,
consumed by all in attendance.
It was a holy meal.

May we find what is holy
in our own awkward journeys
to rivers unknown, kindness
scattered on the water
like leaves, bright and lilting.
May we remember

to cleanse the palate of sin
with eternal mystery.

◊*What prompted this poem is an experience shared by my sister which has stayed with me for several decades. It seemed to provide a symbol for how joining others in a ritual born of their own culture can become a moment of grace, of community, of affirmation of the presence of God, despite our differences.*

Carol Barrett teaches poetry and healing courses for two universities. Her most recent book *Pansies* is the first book in English about the Apostolic Lutheran community, a group of primarily Finnish descent, who forbid birth control. It was a finalist for the 2020 Oregon book awards.

WE ARE ALL GOD'S POEMS
Salena Beaumont Hill, Báawatbakala Xíasseesh (Shining Crucifix)

We are all God's poems
You know how I know this is true?

My dad, he was a poem
He was an Indian Cowboy poem
He was rough and tough on the outside
and sweet and caring on the inside

My dad, he was a poem
He was a teacher
He was full of wisdom and life lessons
and taught us how to love unconditionally

My dad, he was a poem
He was a dad and a poppa
He was full of jokes and stories
and taught us to laugh and to listen
and to be kind and to take care of one another

My dad, he was a poem
He was Baashóop Bachée Itchísh (Chief of Four Deeds)
He was Apsáalooke
and he was spiritual
and he was respectful
and he honored Apsáalooke ways

My dad, he was a poem
He was Akbaatatdía's poem
And he taught me how to be a poem for my children

◊*As an elementary student in Pryor, Montana, I had the great fortune of being a student of the late Mick Fedullo. Mick was a writer and poet who introduced his students to a new form of writing and encouraged our creativity. He was loved and appreciated by many on the Crow Reservation and will forever be remembered by his students. Ever since elementary school, I have always appreciated poetry and have been inspired by Indigenous women poets such as Heather Cahoon and Joy Harjo. The artistry of my three daughters has also influenced me to be brave enough to express my own creativity.*

Salena Beaumont Hill, Báawatbakala Xíasseesh (Shining Crucifix), is a member of the Apsáalooke (Crow) Nation and descendent of the Amaskapi Pikuni (Blackfeet) Nation in Montana. Salena has always loved poetry and has been influenced by the late Mick Fedullo who was a writer and teacher of poetry, and her friend, Heather Cahoon (Confederated Salish and Kootenai Tribes of Montana).

(IF) WE ARE ALL GOD'S POEMS
Katherine Hagopian Berry

how can the lesson for today
be the Ark and the Tabernacle
God of Law, unnamable
who knows a thing and keeps it holy
who erases nuance,
lays out the sacred plan?

Still, there are two arks, one
for rules, one to resist them,
to save what can be saved.
There are two tents, one
to make a gesture of permanence
one born from remainder, the discarded

it is what I bring, not holiest of holies
not sacred, not priest,
not cloth of gold,
not cherubim, wheels or wings
not incense or candle or laver or alter
not bloodred leather, not even the ram.

Just what you gather when you walk out
behind the church on a November evening,
raw sun sinking low on the beeches,

vivid orange, rosepurple, gleaming
before it all ages brown, dropped branches
smooth on your hand, sap pungent like smoke.

Above you the sky is an ocean,
crow could be raven, hope its harsh cry.

Like nest, I build the tabernacle
twig by twig, roofed in what I find,
enough to keep dry, enough to warm hands,
together in shelter, we are all the dove,

enough eyes gleaming
to make angels
of our own observing
the moon hanging huge
like a question,
the embering fire.

◊*I received this prompt just as I was preparing to teach the Ark and the Tabernacle to our Godly Play children's group at my progressive church. The story describes the original house of worship for the Hebrew people, a pretty intricate tent to hold the Ark of the Covenant, which of course got me thinking about the contemporary Jewish practice of tabernacle, or sukkot, building, and the other ark, the one that was about salvation rather than law.*

Katherine Hagopian Berry (she/her) has appeared in the *Café Review*, *Feral*, and *Rust + Moth*, among other places. Her first collection, *Mast Year*, was published in 2020. She is a poetry reader for the *Maine Review*.

(IF) WE ARE ALL GOD'S POEMS
LAUREN BERRY

      then why did the Lord stop writing
            when I opened my hips for Him

to bless them?   My lover kisses my belly
     when it grumbles

           prayers— but no stanzas
    fill this womb. I count

the women in this town
     who so much as look

           in men's eyes and they fill
    with the Lord's lyrics,

line by blessed line. While I track

    my breaks,
they measure meter, symbols. My sister says,

     Today my daughter is a single almond,
         a plum, stolen pomegranate,

     heavy mango, a cantaloupe, a head
         of lettuce, magic pumpkin. The water

     will break, the blood on the doctor's table, fresh
        ink. The next chapter wails
           for milk.

>	Did our God see me and know His craft
> 		was through? Against what
>
> 	do I rhyme
> 	if this is true?

◊*I am fascinated by the spectrum of fertility narratives: while some women have unexpected (even unwanted) pregnancies, others endure a devastating struggle to conceive that can take years. As I have watched friends and family members walk through the process in the past few years, this continuum of experience has captured my imagination. It is my hope that this poem might make even one reader feel less alone in her journey.*

Lauren Berry holds Creative Writing degrees from Florida State University and the University of Houston. Terrance Hayes selected her first collection, *The Lifting Dress* to win the National Poetry Series in 2011. Her second collection, *The Rented Altar*, won the C&R Press Award in poetry in 2019.

WE ARE ALL GOD'S POEMS
CooXooEii Black

I agonize over that age-old question
When is it finished? A cry
revised and revised to enjamb
seamlessly with a jubilee,
like a brown trout hushed into the upriver.

I've come to plenty ends of myself. Found worship
is costly, a year's worth of wages, the polished curves
of an alabaster flask shattered, the aroma lingering
in the rungs of this poem, river residue on the shore,
anointing oil poured out from source to mouth.

Lord, please revise the names of those massacred
at Sand Creek into a song. If I knew those screams
and the lashing of fire on teepees, I'd lay awake at night.
That type of choir would send me into a frenzy, then the smoke
would put me down. Revise our nocturnal fears
into a field of lanterns. Oil and flour revised
into a meal. My ancestors did not need a tablespoon

just a table and a mouth to spoon into. Jesus as bread,
epigraph, and envoi. Lord, you must obsess like a poet.
Do you stare at these lines?
Figure how to make them new?
Lord, that age-old question,
how do you begin again again again

◊*I wrote this poem to express my gratitude for the Lord's grace in sanctifying and purifying me. The journey is beautiful and will continue until Jesus returns. In life, I have seen Him turn my brokenness into strength and beauty, and witnessed the same transformation in the lives of historically oppressed and marginalized Native Americans. As we are made in His image, He continues to refine and add lines to our stories. This poem reflects my deep belief in the transformative power of God's love and grace in our lives.*

CooXooEii Black is an Afro-Indigenous poet from the Wind River Reservation and a member of the Northern Arapaho Tribe. He is the author of *The Morning You Saw a Train of Stars Streaking Across the Sky* (Rattle Foundation, 2022). His work has appeared in multiple publications, including Poetry Magazine, Eco Theo Review, Palette Poetry, and Carve Magazine. Black received his Master of Fine Arts in creative writing from the University of Memphis. His poetry is deeply rooted in his Afro-Indigenous heritage and oral tradition, exploring childhood memories, reservation life, land, and faith.

WE ARE ALL GOD'S POEMS
Kimberly Blaeser

Kawishiwi. Circle of latitude 48° north. Where small chips fly out from the
>furious beak of a pileated.

We are late in crossing and hunger pushes us. All around the inferno of
>autumn blazes, fills even the water with copper. With red bronze
>lemon gold and brightest orange—with swallowed glory.

Even as we feast then on the color, winds of decay resist our paddling, and
>the baring of branches continues. This honeyed air—the last exhale
>of leaves.

Woodpeckers, too, like fire in the trees. *Plunk plunk. Plunk*, then *tick*. The
>head blur unearthing dinner, bark's cache of larvae.

We are in this somewhere.

As leaves, perhaps. Or only their refractions—a rippled image on river. Say
we are the roots, tapping groundwater; the branches, drinking. Or are we the
>manic head, the endless motion searching survival? Who would
>claim the beetle for clan? Hard-shelled and burrowing further into
>darkness. Who eats tree, who kills it.

But watch these layers. Hunger and fullness—too deep for measure.

The skin of the tree broken, open. Insects lifted from winding tunnels. The
bark now a calligraphy of holes. Hollowed, but not empty. Shall I tell you
>nature knows no vacuum—only cycle?

How soon the red squirrel. How soon each tongue hunts. How deep the sap.

Yes—the sweetness.

◊*We spent the fall of 2020 at a water-access cabin in the BWCA region, working remotely. As the tornadic force of the pandemic touched all corners of the human world, attending to the intricacies and cycles of the natural kept us tethered—fed us hope.*

Kimberly Blaeser, former Wisconsin Poet Laureate, is the author of five poetry collections including *Copper Yearning*, *Apprenticed to Justice*, and *Résister en dansant/Ikwe-niimi: Dancing Resistance.* A UW–Milwaukee professor and MFA faculty for the Institute of American Indian Arts in Santa Fe, Blaeser is founding director of In-Na-Po—Indigenous Nations Poets.

WE ARE ALL GOD'S POEMS
Ronda Piszk Broatch

as is the wet dog beneath the apple trees.
    Her eyes are votives, are stones
tumbled for a thousand years
       by the river's fingers.
             The door opened

to her, an invitation, a miracle
    forged between myriad dimensions.
When rubbed together,
       trust is born. We are signatures
          of energy,

iterations of loss, the wound in need
    of healing, that which is whole
aching to be cut open. The dog
       is an ode to god,
            as is the clown

we always feared, her down-
    turned mouth, impossible shoes.
What is delight but a disaster
       in constant remaking, a circular
          mistake,

another word for love
    that has no word. We are the ones
gazing into the heavens, searching for Ursa
       Minor, for Omuamua, Neowise,
          our missing

ancestors, the near quantum
    tardigrade. The black bear
is a poem of perfect need,
        wearing her hunger under the sun
                like a prayer. Tell me,

if we are lost in this world,
    what does the idle grass care,
as long as there are bees and dragonflies,
        water bears and wet dogs stitching their names
                in the spaces between blessings.

◊*From early childhood I've had a love of the cosmos, and my favorite pastime was to contemplate what which held the universe in its pocket. Over the years, as I've studied up on cosmology and quantum mechanics/physics, (although I am no scientist!), my belief in God has evolved from tangible to pure energy. In the poem, I loosely gathered in words and surrealist questions to add surprise, and just let the poem come as poems often do.*

Poet and photographer, Ronda Piszk Broatch is the author of *Lake of Fallen Constellations*, (MoonPath Press, 2015). Ronda is the recipient of an Artist Trust GAP Grant, and her poems have been nominated for the Pushcart prize. Her journal publications include *Blackbird, Diagram, Sycamore Review, Missouri Review, Palette Poetry*, and Public Radio KUOW's *All Things Considered*, among others.

WE ARE ALL GOD'S POEMS
AARON BROWN

We sing belonging from our balconies,
strum healing from our violin strings.

When in the months we taped close
picnic tables, watched others

through rolled-up car windows—
it was as if we plugged our ears

and stopped hearing the humming
from our human heaven song.

Stopped seeing the knee come down
on a God-child's neck. Stopped feeling

the richness of kaleidoscopic skin.
But there is a prayer in the sun

that sears everyone the same.
There is a prayer in the ventilator

that channels the breath of God
despite the night. There is a prayer

in what we pushed past the pain—a poem.
Poiema means something made,

and what is there to craft but love,
what is there to sing but a song,

a gut-felt, bone-thrummed psalm
that is a song we keep on singing,

a poem we keep on bringing into being.

◊*Writing a poem wrestling with hope is perhaps the most difficult challenge a poet can undertake without sounding trite or sentimental. But it is a practice that is necessary and needed. I immediately thought of this world that has been given to us post-2020--how it has revealed our vices but it has also revealed our loves. I want to focus on the things we make to push back the darkness.*

Aaron Brown is the author of the poetry collection, *Acacia Road*, winner of the 2016 Gerald Cable Book Award (Silverfish Review Press, 2018) and of the memoir, *Less Than What You Once Were* (Unsolicited Press, 2022). He has published work in *Prairie Schooner*, *Image*, *World Literature Today online*, *Waxwing*, and *Transition*, among others, and he is a contributing editor for *Windhover*. Brown grew up in Chad and now lives in Texas, where he is an assistant professor of English and directs the writing center at LeTourneau University. He holds an MFA from the University of Maryland.

WE ARE ALL GOD'S POEMS—MISSIONS
Heather Cahoon

From our house in Indian town
we can see the old brick mission,
its outline red against the mountains.
Outside are three small wind-worn cabins
whose walls are held together with bleak
and yellowed photographs of the church
surrounded by hundreds of tipis.
>All those tipis have been turned
>to HUD houses, the trails paved,
>chiefs Charlo and Arlee are now
>just names of nearby towns.

Though I came for information,
wanting to know about the boarding school,
Agnes told me about her day.
She asked about my older sister
and her baby, where they were living now.
She heard they'd moved off the reservation.
>We talked all afternoon and sometimes
>she'd speak so softly I had to close
>my eyes to hear.

Agnes said that many who believed
the fathers' teachings allowed
their minds to become numb and they act
as if someone has stolen their tongues.
>Maybe they believed too much, because
>like Samson, when their hair was cut off
>they lost strength.

Until the fear of living, the fear of dying,
the fear the teachings instilled

has been abandoned, until that fear
has bled from every color in their eyes
they will be lost.
> They will remain like fields of wheat
> that tumble over themselves
> on endless missions to find grace

◊ *'Missions' stems from a handful of related incidents--growing up in tribal housing where I saw the St. Ignatius Mission out my bedroom window, spending time browsing those old photographs inside those cabins (which I believe were the priests' headquarters/ living area and now house relevant memorabilia and are open to the public in the summers as little museums), learning more about the assimilation era of federal Indian policy as a student at UM, and then going home to interview an elder about the boarding school. Ultimately, the advent of Christianity brought significantly more hardships to the tribal people than it did blessings--primary among the negative impacts was the resulting loss of tribal cultural knowledge, hence the final stanza of the poem. 'Missions' is from the chapbook Elk Thirst (University of Montana Press, 2005).*

Heather Cahoon, PhD, earned her MFA in poetry from the University of Montana, where she was the Richard Hugo Scholar. She has received a Potlatch Fund Native Arts Grant and Montana Arts Council Artist Innovation Award. Her chapbook, *Elk Thirst*, won the Merriam-Frontier Prize. Her book of poems *Horsefly Dress* appears with University of Arizona Press. She is an assistant professor of Native American studies at the University of Montana. She is from the Flathead Reservation and is a member of the Confederated Salish and Kootenai Tribes.

WE ARE ALL GOD'S POEMS
Andrew J. Calis

Easter, 2021

My Teta nearly cries, then does. She
is old, and she has missed us. The lines
she speaks and *is* are one, and we
can do nothing — paralyzed by love.

We stand there, deaf to the words that speak to her;
blinded by the light in her eyes; *this
is life*, I think she says. Or,
this is right. She will not define *this*,

of course. We already know, or never
will, the caverns of herself. The dark
there, the black worry that she would never
see us again. The panics of her heart.

But it is Easter now. And she can put
to sleep those worries, or at least keep
them quiet. This new joy will not be shut
in, will not rest, is loud and echoing,
this spring light, stone-shattering, echoing
a newness that will not rest, that spreads like roots
beneath damp ground, soaks in life, seeps
life into its veins, grows like truth —

too thick to shake, remade and echoing
Lazarus's rise from four days' sleep,
and the hollow of the cave that made Christ weep.

◊*In the poem, I try to connect the personal sadness of my grandmother during quarantine to a universal isolation (linking her tears to Christ's who lost a friend), and in this way, show the unity of the human experience of suffering via loneliness. But suffering thankfully comes to an end, and there's hope in the resurrection, which in many ways is a return to the joy of community.*

Andrew J. Calis is a Palestinian-American poet and father of four wonderful kids. His first book of poetry, *Pilgrimages* (2020), was praised by James Matthew Wilson for having "the intensity of Hopkins" and for "layer[ing] light on light in hopes of helping us to see." He lives, writes, and teaches near Baltimore, MD.

WE ARE ALL GOD'S POEMS
Mary Ann Clute

I have only guessed at the darkness
you have seen with innocent eyes
my tears join yours as you rage
overwhelmed by fear, anger, and sorrow
there are not words for your pain
I never understood what each syllable
of the word DE-SO-LA-TION meant
until your sobs reverberated against my ribs.

When you hold your arms up
my heart melts
I see the spark still in your eyes as the
tears dry
you stop to watch the flight of birds
you study the ripples you make in the puddle
with the stick you wield like a sword
you shout with joy at the spray of water
as you stick your fingers up the waterspout
of the tub.

We will not let the shattered rearview mirror of the past
continue to reflect and distort
we will join hands to hold you and love you
until the shadows fade.

◊*Foster children are truly God's poems! I was blessed to provide respite care for my daughter's two year old foster son over six months. It is looking like he has found a forever home and we continue to be blessed to be involved in his life.*

Mary Ann Clute is an Emeritus Social Work Professor from Eastern Washington University. She finished her clinical career at Hospice of Spokane. Her greatest joys are now grandparenting, running and writing. The little one above is a grandchild of her heart.

WE ARE ALL GOD'S POEMS
Nan Cohen

Some of the poems are sick.
For them, breathing is suddenly work.

Some of the poems are well for now.
They sit near the bed and talk.

Or pace the hospital hallway or call
and get choked up on the phone.

Some are far away, thinking of you.
Some are wishing they could cure cancer.

And some of them are nurses,
whose work is to access the plastic port

implanted just below the collarbone,
pushing a needle into that tiny heart.

◊ *I found myself browsing the many entries in my commonplace book about what poetry is and what it can do. So many of them seemed to have something to say about the ways in which we might be "all God's poems," but the one that most spoke to me in the moment was from an interview with Donald Hall, in which he cited an essay by the physician and writer Jed Myers, recommending "the pragmatically useless treatment called poetry, whereby we might leave our patients less alone when our medicine leaves us all alone." Thinking of the way we can be companioned in hard moments by a person or by a poem was my avenue into this poem.*

Nan Cohen, the longtime poetry director of the Napa Valley Writers' Conference, is the author of two books of poems, *Rope Bridge* (2005) and *Unfinished City* (2017). The recipient of a Wallace Stegner Fellowship and a Literature Fellowship from the NEA, she lives in Los Angeles.

WE ARE ALL GOD'S POEMS
Matt Daly

Sagebrush buttercups rise up
right after the snowbanks

melt. Snow again falls and suddenly
juncos. If you cannot picture
yellow flowers shining in moldy grass

or the tails of juncos streaking whitely
over frail, new drifts, don't

look them up. Look up tonight

toward the group of stars called sisters

by some of us. I will find you
out in the wild dark, for this rewilding world

has a voice like a pole, and our own
rewilding cells quiver into bands.
Even if you are in an arc far from my arc,

speak in your verse, for we can turn
to each other as wildness returning.

◊ *I find solace in the wild world. In relation with wild lives, I feel the enlivening bigness of bigger forces more clearly than in the human-made world. I feel how the cells of me are wild and are in the steady process of remaking. This feels like hope: to be part of wildness remaking itself. And so I try to feel how language is also a wild and alive part of how we honor the bigness that enlivens us.*

Matt Daly is the author of *Between Here and Home* (Unsolicited Press) and the chapbook *Red State* (Seven Kitchens Press). He is a recipient of the Neltje Blanchan Award for writing inspired by the natural world and a Creative Writing Fellowship in Poetry from the Wyoming Arts Council.

WE ARE ALL GOD'S POEMS
Dawson Davenport

In the reflection of my grandfather's eye
Cloaked in my ancestor's garb
I echo the chambers
Of remnants of
Song
Dance
And a labor of love
Lost
Language
Caressing the hardships
Of today's abuser
Crying silently as
I see my 16 year old self
Shuffled away down a
Cold corridor
Not knowing the journey in store
But in the sacred fire of my soul
I knew that my grandfather was there
In the writings on the wall
The stories told
The smell of bleach
And dead hopes
Lingered through the
Revolving
Rays of sun
That sometimes
Snuck through the
Bulletproof windows
I knew my grandfather's
Presence
Was imminent

As the cold gates closed behind me
Nothing is permanent
Except that my grandfather
Was a pilot
Who would have flown Buddy Holly,
And Ritchie Valens and
The Big Bopper
If the storm wasn't as bad
My grandfather was there

And it is in this reflection
That I've learned to know
It's that
We are all gods' poems

◊*This poem was inspired by my creator, Kettimaneto, and my biological grandfather, C.B Davenport, WWII veteran US NAVY, who became a private pilot after his service. He was supposed to fly the musicians but was overrode by a pilot with more experience in severe weather.*

Dawson Davenport is a member of the Meskwaki Nation.

WE ARE ALL GOD'S POEMS
Noah Davis

Three days of horse trails
cross the white pasture
and I have yet to find
an hour to follow them
over the cheek of the hill
to the teeth of the tree line
where they huddle before dark
to shovel the snow
with their hooves for dying
grass, which is an image
of hunger rewritten
in every belly
no matter what
the throat swallows.

◊ *Poetry is engrained in form, and when I think about God as creator, I think about the form of the world. The trails all of us creatures leave here on the earth. The shape of our bodies and the landscape. The need to consume to retain our form. All of this is holy because it's of this sacred world.*

Noah Davis grew up in Tipton, Pennsylvania, and writes about the Allegheny Front. Davis' book of poems, *Of This River* (August 2020), was selected by George Ella Lyon for the Wheelbarrow Emerging Poet Book Prize from Michigan State University's Center for Poetry. Davis earned an MFA from Indiana University and now lives with his wife, Nikea, in Missoula, Montana.

WE ARE ALL GOD'S POEMS
TODD DAVIS

The pad
of a bear's
paw
slips
through mud
and ash
along
the stream
clouded
with last year's
fires.

By July
the banks
flower
with purple
flame,
fireweed
claiming
the ground
of its
birth.

The only
poems
I care about
in this
hour
are the fish
that tail
downstream

for water
clear
enough
to breathe.

All our mothers
took the first
breath
as we swam
toward them,
sweet gods
who resurrected
us.

◊*I spend a great deal of time in wild spaces, away from humans and the worlds we've constructed that scar and smother the gift of the first, primal earth. While I see God in the faces and bodies of other humans—and give thanks for this—I'm most drawn to the presence of God in other animals, other forms of life found in the woods and waters of my home place. In these spaces I often find myself dwelling on birth and its mirror image, death, which reminds me of all creators, all mothers and ancestors—including my own—who give life.*

Todd Davis is the author of six books of poetry, most recently *Native Species* and *Winterkill*, both published by Michigan State University Press. He's won the Foreword INDIES Book of the Year Bronze and Silver Awards, the Midwest Book Award, and the Bloomsburg University Book Prize. He teaches environmental studies at Pennsylvania State University's Altoona College.

WE ARE ALL GOD'S POEMS
Carmen dela Cruz

I have witnessed this,
some twenty hours
laboring for a miracle,
faces coming in and out,
nurses, doctors, your father
holding my legs, counting,
everyone calling,
daring me to push, push, push once more,
three, four hours,
a crown of black hair
but you would not yet shine,

silently crying,
for my mother in heaven,
the pain, I can't go on,
then a flurry of footsteps,
a doctor's precise cut,
you emerge from below my belly,
I cannot hold you,
God's valiant helpers still working on me,
I'm trembling, from exhaustion, cold, and lost
blood, but I can hear it,
a strong cry, a sound so glorious,
bursting forth,
my son, you are God's poem,
a mixed verse, from your Filipino Dad,
and Black Mom,
you are a part of me, us,
but you are a beautiful song, all your own,
the moment you are in my arms,
nursing at my breast,

I feel nothing but the divine.

◊*I was thinking of the recent birth of my son. After all the trauma my body went through, there was this moment of awe, hearing this tiny human for the first time. I am God's creation, but here I am as God's instrument, bringing this new poem, new verse, into the world.*

Carmen dela Cruz has an MFA in Creative Writing from Chatham University. She is enrolled in Gonzaga University's Doctorate in Leadership Studies program. Her poem "The Silent Fight" was recently published in *Black Visions: a Jeffery "Boosie" Bolden Anthology*. Her essay Selma: An Exploration of the Womanist Lens and the Servant-Leader was first included in the 2020 edition of the *International Journal of Servant-Leadership* and was more recently included in *Servant-Leadership, Feminism, and Gender Well-Being*, published in September of 2022 by SUNY Press.

WE ARE ALL GOD'S POEMS
Shruti Desai

My eyes,
tongue, skin, ears,
and nose—
they are sounds
so enlivened
by the dirt of the earth
that I emerged
in the laughter of their play. My life,
an echo
of remembrance—the past inside the present,
snaking its silent hiss
into the vessels
of my human abode,
where the future
is a stream
of life-giving
redemption: honor me, I pray,
in all the luminescent poetry
of the forgotten ways,
cradle my torment,
till I remember
how to breathe;
stop me
before I drown
in the cacophonies
of unkindness and heart-ripping
pain, dripping
from vials of stored up tears—
the regret engraved
upon the shadows of haste
where I crossed my innocence

and railed against my own worth,
extinguishing the flame of my sacred fire.
When I thought it was too late
to come back to life,
I learned there's no such thing
in the library of God's mind,
for in the bellowing mists of time,
a prayer back to love
whispers a distant light:
may I learn to unwrite the story of what once was,
and treasure the beauty of my endless making.

◊*This poem grew out of steeping in the sorrow and pain that I feel when I remember the ways I forsake what was here, given to me. Writing the poem helped me make contact with tenderness, love, and sacredness, which shine despite my stories and experiences of the past, offering a way to forgive myself and all that happened and to reconnect with self, body, and life.*

Shruti Desai is an artist, writer, and researcher interested in human-nature relationships and the power of creativity to imagine more compassionate and nourishing ways to live together. She writes and creates to remember what is worth living and caring for.

WE ARE ALL GOD'S POEMS
A. Eagleshield

Lakȟól'iya imáčhaǧe šni, k'éyaš mičhíŋča kiŋ yámni lakȟótiya
        wóglakapi okíhipi kta čha lakȟól'iya uŋspémič'ičhiye.
Eháŋk'ehaŋ uŋtȟúŋpi šni itȟókab wičháhuŋkake kiŋ otákuye kiŋ
        owás'iŋ thekíčhiȟilapi.
Uŋčí Makȟá na Tȟuŋkášila kiŋ slolkíyapi.
Wičháhuŋkake k'uŋ iyápi waŋ wakȟáŋ čha iyápi na eháŋni wičhóȟ'aŋ kiŋ
gluhápi na Wamákȟaškaŋ oyáte kiŋ iyuha ób
        wičháni.
Uŋčí Makȟá wičháhuŋkake k'uŋ owás'iŋ taŋyéȟči wówičhakič'u.
Aŋpétu kiŋ lé blihénič'iyapi na Iyápi nitȟáwapi kiŋ na eháŋni
        wičhóȟ'aŋ kiŋ wičáyalapi kte héčha.
Iyápi nitȟáwapi kiŋ na eháŋni wičhóȟ'aŋ kiŋ nič'íksuyapi háŋtaŋš
        uŋkítȟakožakpakupi kiŋ owás'iŋ Iyápi nitȟáwapi kiŋ
        wóglakapi na eháŋni wičhóȟ'aŋ kiŋ úŋpi kte.
Waúŋšiwala čha oyúškeya waúŋ.
Wawáčhi čha oyúškeya waúŋ.
Čhéwakiye čha oyúškeya waúŋ.
Wačháŋtwakiya čha oyúškeya wáuŋ.
Oyáte kiŋ nípi kta čha léčhamuŋ.
Mitákuye Owás'iŋ

I didn't grow up speaking Lakota… but I taught myself so my three
        babies could speak their language.
Long ago before we were born, the ancestors and every single one of their
        relations loved each other.
They knew their Grandmother Earth and their Grandfathers (spirits).
Those ancestors spoke a language that is sacred, (and) they held their
        ancient traditions, and they lived with all the nations that live upon
        the earth.

Grandmother Earth provided thoroughly for all of those ancestors.
Today you must take care and believe in your language and lifeways.
If you remember your language and lifeways, all of your grandchildren
       will talk your language and exist through the lifeways.
When I'm compassionate, I'm free.
When I dance, I'm free.
When I pray, I'm free.
When I love with no bounds, I'm free.
I do this so the people will live.
We're all related.

◊*My ancestors spoke a language that was sacred. Because of them I love with no bounds.*

A. Eagleshield is a Lakota poet.

WE ARE ALL GOD'S POEMS
Charles Finn

We are all God's poems
The black man on the corner
In his best Sunday suit and tie
The Asian woman picking up her mail
The gay couple in the park
Wedding bands lit by the sun.

There is the Native boy
Riding his bicycle to play basketball
His best friend double behind him.
There is the man from Senegal
Tying his shoe on the subway
Free verse if ever there was
And the woman from Mexico City
Laughing with her sister in perfect rhyme.

There is the homeless man asleep in the doorway
Almost pastoral, and the Muslim on his prayer rug.
There is the junkie with a pretty smile
The prostitute with a pretty smile
The refugee in Syria
With a pretty smile
All of them a narrative worth repeating.

There is the newborn with Down Syndrome
A beautiful haiku, and the girl at the checkout with braces
A couplet with the bagboy with acne
His mother a sonnet in the senior living facility
Trying to recall his name.

Turn the page, we are all God's poems
Lyric, epic, you a ballad
Me a limerick, every last one of us dogeared and coffee-stained
And every last one of us a love poem, just look
At the anthology we make.

◊*Just days after the Capital building in Washington D.C. was stormed by rioters, co-editor Shann Ray commented on a Facebook post, saying "We are all God's poems." I'd left the Catholic church years ago and I struggle with the idea of a personified God, but the phrase struck me as incredibly beautiful, wonderfully poetic, and I told him it'd make a great title to a poem. I even dashed off a few lines, the very first of which survive above. A few more exchanges, a phone call, and an hour later the idea for this anthology was born. As for the poem, I wanted to say that even the most ordinary among us is beautiful and worthy of love, no matter our skin color, where we were born, economic background, sexual preferences, religious beliefs. At some point the idea to link people to the different styles of poetry occurred to me, but the trick was to make sure I wasn't being too cute. I didn't want the weight of the original idea diluted by my play on words. In the end, I'd like to think I struck a reasonable balance.*

Charles Finn in the author of *Wild Delicate Seconds: 29 Wildlife Encounters*, *On a Benediction of Wind: Poems a Photographs from the American West*, (winner of the 2022 Montana Book Award) and co-editor of *The Art of Revising Poetry: 21 U.S. Poets on Their Drafts, Craft, and Process*.

WE ARE ALL GOD'S POEMS
Natalya Fisher

I put my hand on your chest
You cried out
it burns

I don't know why I
touch the marks on your skin

Please cradle my cheek in your scar creases

I carve your name into my palms

You said my hand burned you
the way
iron graven into ivory
imprints me the sister

Who thinks her anger saves
but forgets to remove
the world's pain

Do you know that I love you

Trace the lines on the inside
of your hand
the right makes a mountain
the left a river

A black alabaster crucifix
hangs above the piano

in the living room of the house
I grew up in

In your palms an open wound

Your hands like water

◊*I am a voice teacher to students ranging in years from 7 to 81. From this vocation, I have learned how vulnerable and sacred our voices are. Singing requires intense courage and deep surrender to allow a teacher to critique and analyze one's voice. This poem arose out of contemplating how together with God we might carry our sorrow, our generational patterns, and our dreams in our bodies and how I find solace in the touch of the beloved: my husband, my family, and the Divine.*

Natalya Fisher is an artist and collaborator currently living in New York City. In professional regional theaters she has played Lynette "Squeaky" Fromme in Sondheim's *Assassins*, the Soothsayer in Shakespeare's *Julius Caesar*, and Jo March in Louisa May Alcott's *Little Women*.

WE ARE ALL GOD'S POEMS
Kathleen Flenniken

Because I had agreed to hold the man's place in line while he left to fetch
    his cane
he paid me back in his booming voice with his memoirs.
The line went out the door of the Post Office—Valentine's rush—and he
    covered
a lot of ground while we waited six feet apart (less, but what could I do)

including his seven college majors and the failure of Darwin to describe
a world that God created in six days (his friend with a Nobel Prize agreed)
followed by his martial arts class with Bruce Lee who was so fast
he'd exchange the quarter in each of his palms for two dimes and a nickel
and you couldn't even see his arms move. That's pretty fast

I said. His mask was a complicated whole-head affair
that made him look like a welder or a guy stuck inside a mailbox.
He explained he'd had a brain stroke and ever since if he fell down
he couldn't get up. The stroke hadn't dampened his voice.

He'd been head lifeguard at the U of W, and when he was 59
he could still walk five miles in 1:02 before he boxed a few rounds
then warmed down with a mile swim.

The pretty-seeming woman ahead of me holding a comically tall stack of
    parcels
turned around once to meet my eyes.

I offered when he asked that I hailed from Eastern Washington.
He'd had a great-grandfather from there he met just twice, when he was three
and the man was 103, and when he was seven, and the man was 107.
He lived to be 112 but his brothers lived to 114, 116, and 118. And 120.

Everybody else in line stayed quiet and I believed I was their representative,
ready to receive whatever the man had to share. Then it was my turn
at the counter but for a few minutes longer there we were in our masks
and orderly distances in the shadow of Bruce Lee's dangerous hands—
every one of us on the honor system, the most honorable system of all the
        systems.

◊*In another time I don't know how I might have reacted to a stranger launching into his life story in a slow-moving line, but for now I need my human connections where I can find them. He had a big voice and it became a communal experience, which felt important.*

Kathleen Flenniken is the author of three poetry collections: *Post Romantic* (University of Washington Press, 2020), *Plume* (2012) and *Famous* (2006). She served as Washington State Poet Laureate from 2012-2014.

WE ARE ALL GOD'S POEMS
Joy Gaines-Friedler

She cut her hair. Long curls gone to the floor
along with something else, something – companionable.
Bravely she let it go. A liberation of sorts. The way
grandma once told a man I smoke because it God damn
pleases me. Frightened, discharged into the world, she
is alone, a figure in a painting, examined
for what she represents, examined for what she instills.

Mouths say it all. They often shut tight. Some people lie, others
mean it when they say they love it, or worse – a fear
on their faces as though she is a mirror. We are scared,
uncertain, we cling to mortal youth & beauty. That thing,
that vibrant thing that shapes the soul, gets us invited
to the party, causes wars. No. She sees it now

the long curls gone to the floor will be swept away,
but what is left, is this face—this beautiful face—lit,
seen, maybe for the first time, empty, willing, unlabeled,
so perfectly imperfect.

◊*When I thought of the writing prompt We Are All God's Poems, a two-word phrase came to mind: crossing over, and how a poem is the mechanism by which we do exactly that; we cross over into understanding ourselves more fully, and without judgement. All things are transitory, especially beauty, and self-love. But beauty defined by what, and by whom?*

Joy Gaines-Friedler is the author of three books of poetry including the award-winning *Capture Theory*. Joy teaches for non-profits in the Detroit area, including Freedom House Detroit where she teaches poetry to asylum seekers from western and northern Africa. Widely published, Joy is a multiple Pushcart Prize nominated poet.

WE ARE ALL GOD'S POEMS
Makoto Fujimura

My chickens live with question
marks
on their feathers
and in their vermillion eyes.

Whether the quest be
of ants crawling
on a wooden plank
or red tails circling
above, or clovers waving
beyond the fencing.

These are all questions
that can only be
pecked at, or by
standing perfectly still,
as the hawk circling cannot perceive
them if they remain unmoved.

As I do now, watching them.

And upon midday,
the laying of an egg
is giving little births
full of rituals
and exhortations.

But who determines
their fate?

What quests
fortify them from
their Flights?

The rhythm of their
delight and agitated
dance, wrapped in their
naive instinct to Live or Love

Fully clothed and comfortable
without answers or certainties;
the imperishable contained
in the patterns of their feathered
gyrations.

◊*Being at my farm in Princeton (what I call affectionately "Fuji Farm"), I had been raising chickens for a while and learned quite a bit from them. This poem is a free verse that I often write as a form of observation, like my many sketches of plants and birds around the farmland.*

Makoto Fujimura is a leading contemporary artist whose process-driven, refractive "slow art" has been described by David Brooks of the New York Times as "a small rebellion against the quickening of time". After being nominated by President Obama, he served on the National Arts Council. He is the author of *Silence and Beauty*.

WE ARE ALL GOD'S POEMS
Kem Gambrell

On all fours
I crawl into her womb
Mother' dwelling
of willow and blanket.
The scent of her haven greets me.

Quiet

Sitting in the dark abyss
one by one
glowing stones carried in
wrapping me in warmth.

Still

Ladles of water poured onto the rocks
the ancestors clacking in retort
Steam engulfing
cleanses and purifies.

Listen

Song prayer begins
reconnecting me to
home
self
earth
loved ones.

My separateness
frustration

dejection
and ego
Slide away, dripping from my body
as the stones dim and the haze dissipates.

Peace

Traveling full circle
I crawl out
whole again.

◊*Influence: The first time I had the profound honor of participating in a sweat lodge, it changed my life. The four elements, connection to Mother Earth, prayer songs, and the reminder of deep unbreakable connection transformed how I thought about relationship to everything. Decades and hundreds of lodges later, I continue to be deeply humbled by the power of the space and this way of prayer and connection.*

Kem Gambrell is a seventh-generation white settler from the United States. She is a scholar, educator, and perpetual student seeking to fully embody and incorporate a decolonial mindset. She teaches in the leadership program at Gonzaga University and her focus includes diverse ways of being, studies, Indigenous ways of relationship, and social construction.

WE ARE ALL GOD'S POEMS (WHERE EELS SPAWN)

Michael Garrigan

For years no one knew where eels went to spawn once they left their rivers. For years they disappeared. For years they simply vanished then reappeared as small slivers sliding back into their freshwater homes. Finally, someone tracked one and found them in the Sargasso Sea where the four Atlantic currents collide - the Gulf Stream from the east, the Canary from the west, the North Atlantic and Equatorial from the North and South - and drop the detritus of their land, clockwise, growing into a clear blue ocean graveyard gyre of seaweed and eel. I bet you could find the DNA of every living thing in that sea. Something died, something ate it, something decomposed, water came, washed it to sea. Eels spawn where our deaths lie, bringing back a little bit of us when they return to their rivers. We are maps of each other. It's easy to forget just how much water we are made of and perhaps it's our shared faith in it that keeps us afloat.

The Sargasso Sea's
bordered by holy currents
holding all of us.

◊*I wrote this poem in direct response to the prompt* We Are All God's Poems *which compelled me to consider what universal faith we have in common.*

Michael Garrigan writes and teaches along the Susquehanna River in Pennsylvania and believes that every watershed should have a Poet Laureate. He is the author of two poetry collections, *Robbing the Pillars* and the chapbook *What I Know [How to Do]*.

(WE ARE ALL GOD'S POEMS) THE FOUNDRESS
Caitlin Smith Gilson

Exquisitely unarmed in the estuary of the eternal
She said:
>	I am within this life of Yours
>	Yours curled and carved and convened a sunlit heat within mine
>	To shine
>	To shine
>	To shine into the depths of earth and bone
>	Colder than winter's snow

The many chambered silence of heart and womb
Foreclosed our ancient tomb
The designated passenger
The bearer of all time
Redressed our guilt with unfinished gentleness
Lain on grass

In the dying
Titans heave the imperishable and are forcibly pulled in two
Essence thrown aside
Flesh collapsing like worn clothes kicked to the floor
We know nothing of what it means to surrender the ghost

Irremediably unprepared for what has shattered within each of us
And unstudied in the unrelenting gentleness
Pressing itself into our remaining shape and time
Whittling itself down along the line
Lowered through the veil of every generation
Pressed and dried hillside flowers

Pushed aside books and shuffled photographs forfeiting all recollection
Hushed into the many chambered corners of failure and love
His body and blood
In Her body and blood
In our body and blood
Transmuting the grave
Redeem us in our unreadiness
Our Lord of the Lost and Found

◊*What influenced the poem: my father experienced a long and heartrending death. He lived with us and we with him, together in that exhausting, daily intensity of love and hopes whittled down into weakness and resignation, of childlike, holy faith carving the dying, and a relentless march towards the end. So much, and in ways that I haven't yet learned, has it pressed into me the spiritual force of dying.*

Caitlin Smith Gilson is Professor of Philosophy at University of Holy Cross, New Orleans. She is the author of several books, most recently her poetry collection *Tregenna Hill: Altars & Allegories* (2021).

WE ARE ALL GOD'S POEMS
Diane Glancy

Then an angel of the Lord said to Philip, Get up and go toward the south to the road that goes down from Jerusalem to Gaza. (This is a wilderness road.)
— *Acts 8:26*

He found in his grandmother's house a jar labeled *threads too short for using*.
The threads a wilderness road before he disappeared back to his Father in
    heaven.
The left the Holy Crusades.
The religious schools where Indian children died.
The horrendous history of Christianity to be reckoned with.
Yet he came for the poverty of threads.
The remaindered.
Kept in a jar.
Labeled as such.
He traveled among those who believed.
Threads lengthened by his hand.

◊*I am from a saving, sparing people who came from the Depression.* **We must be sparing**. *It is a statement that haunts my work.*

Diane Glancy's recent books include *Island of the Innocent, a Consideration of the Book of Job*; *A Line of Driftwood, the Ada Blackjack Story*; and *Home is the Road, Wandering the Land, Shaping the Spirit*. An anthology, *Unpapered*, is also forthcoming. Glancy is professor emerita at Macalester College.

WE ARE ALL GOD'S POEMS
Karen Gookin

That his gaze goes straight
to the Host he raises, that his words
come slow with intention, that his
voice rings clear and sure
as he wipes the Cup, caressing
each drop of Sacred. That his robes
seem to lift and float when he strides
from the altar—so much so
that I must reach out, must answer
the ancient longing to touch
just the cloak
of this believer. I'll sing, too,
as he hands me along.

◊*My poem was inspired when my husband and I attended a friend's First Mass (one of a Catholic priest's first actions after he is newly ordained). The mystery and joy we experienced during Father Thomas Aquinas' (O.P.) First Mass reminded me of the need many have—as Walker Percy portrayed in one of his novels—to rely on someone whose deep faith upholds our own weak belief.*

Karen Gookin grew up in the wheat country of Northern Montana. Her poetry considers family life in that expansive land and in the shrub steppes of Washington, where she lives now. She and her husband, both retired professors and musicians, enjoy reading, writing, family, gardening, fly fishing, travel, and prayer.

WE ARE ALL GOD'S POEMS
Tami Haaland

for Philip

Each day we hike into wildness edging the city. Trails
        wind and converge. Humans follow deer trails,
    deer step over human prints. Ants migrate through sage
        and sand, which allows them to make their own
            small city each spring.

Gnarled and twisted pines mark the way, their roots
        surrounded by stone. Tree bodies choose to lie down
    or lean into each other. In one place a hawthorn, its ripe berries
        hanging in dark clusters, nearby a ponderosa where a single
            magpie watches.

I love each step, the influx, the way boulders split
        into uneven pieces when a juniper seeds itself on top.
    And when we return home, the mountain ash, the last to let go
        its leaves this fall, even on cloudy days seems to glow
            with light.

◊*Over the past several years, I've spent many days on the trails near my house, falling in love with the trees that mark the way, the nuances of seasons and microclimate, of animal encounters. From childhood, hiking has been my method for calming the interior and finding a sense of expansive wonder. This poem originated in response to good advice—to focus more narrowly—but the speaker chooses expansiveness before coming to dwell on a single image at the end. How to think about the title has been both difficult and simple. I am always thinking about God and always deeply aware of human limitations in comprehending.*

Tami Haaland is the author of three poetry collections, most recently *What Does Not Return*. Her poems have appeared in *The American Journal of Poetry*, *The Ecopoetry Anthology*, and *Healing the Divide*. Her work has been featured on *The Slowdown*, *The Writer's Almanac*, *Verse Daily*, and *American Life in Poetry*.

WE ARE ALL GOD'S POEMS —
Travis Helms

smoke coaxed from incense, babbling of birds
and beasts ascending in the east each evening,

rinsing the horizon rim wider and more brightly,
leavening the west. Confess a pain still aching

in the veins, a signature unregistered
deep down in the bone and loam of things.

I have no right to write about these things, I
think. Mists of wistfulness and waking angst

alight against again the fall — and, over it all:
a quiet luminescence wanting to elide the white-

ness effloresces. Smoke stoked from incense,
bones of beasts, the pressured freshness, yes,

the feeling of your fingers in the ground, making
traceless shapes within the dust, hieroglyphing

each of the myths we've lost, we've missed. Sin,
for the desert saints, was taken from a term

for archery: the mark we miss, not some ancient
influenza stinking in our genes. Dream distances.

Speak peace. The heart, when it finally breaks,
breaks softly: a wake of tears, the motor of the boat

switched off: the surface of a blue balloon pushed
past the stress that it can bear: the garish glare of

gums from a barely aware infant, who's yet to cut
a tooth. She wants to bite it to oblivion,

my daughter, flourishing the bouquet of balloons
an aunt has gifted her like a flaming sword. Or

like Goethe's last words upon his deathbed:
more light. Or Hopkins': I am so happy (twice).

I loved my life. Or whatever words, by god, we are
holding to and with and forth — inside this hard, un-

ending, this everything-upending sleight of night.

◊ *This poem began for me as an exercise in hospitality: in thinking about ways of infusing a bit more oxygen into the stanza — of aerating the page in order to give the reader more space to breathe and move through. I have recently been captivated by the Greek Orthodox theologian Alexander Schmemann's notion that the work of every human being is to celebrate all that exists in the created world as sacred, in the way that a priest celebrates the Eucharist. This poem was my effort to hymn all that my eye alights upon in its blessed givenness.*

Travis Helms is author of *Blowing Clover, Falling Rain: a theological commentary on the poetic canon of the 'American Religion'* (Wipf & Stock). An Episcopal priest based in Jackson, WY, he is founder + curator of LOGOS: a liturgically-inflected reading series and project of EcoTheo Collective.

WE ARE ALL GOD'S POEMS
Rachael Henry

— My Daughters: The Sun and The Moon

I remember when I was a little girl
I felt God in the arms of my mother
When she tucked my hair behind my ear
as she sung me to sleep

She was The Music
And now it's my turn to sing

I've been told that children are sacred
because they are the closest to God
I feel God through them
More than any other

I was given The Sun and The Moon
Sacred little ones
Who hold my hand and heal my soul
And I get to be their mother

The Moon exudes unbridled joy
Her fearlessness proclaimed by her scars

The Sun listens
And speaks with compassion that humbles me

I am The Song
Filled with emotion
Singing through motherhood

They need me to be strong
I am not
They need me to be patient
I am not

Strong women before
Strong women ahead
How do I become the bridge?

They lead me through each of their journeys
Going two places at the same time
That test my patience and make my voice falter
And yet when they fall asleep in my arms each night
I cry tears of love from the depths of my soul

Motherhood is a love that spins with such chaos
I can't always see the beauty until we are both still

It took becoming a mother for me to feel God again
To embrace the sacred in my arms
And lift them up to their place in the sky
As The Sun and The Moon

I was given The Sun and The Moon
Sacred little ones
Who hold my hand and heal my soul
And I get to be their mother

I've been told that children are sacred
because they are the closest to God
I feel God through them
More than any other

◊*Her daughters are named after the sun and the moon. They are her inspiration for this poem.*

Rachael Henry is an enrolled member of the Cheyenne River Sioux Tribe. Her Lakota name, Wicaglate Win, was given to her by her Grandfather which he translated as Lady Singer.

WE ARE ALL GOD'S POEMS
José Hernandez

This is supposed to be the land of the free
Where people reach out with helping hands,
And see others around
Able to find what they seek,
Caricuao, black horse, subway, Caracas,

In a wonderful world full of deceit
That promises all but what they want to be,
White rice, black beans, simple metal spoon, my father's gray teeth.
A singer, a doctor, an artist or a baker, indeed

This is supposed to be the land of the brave,
A Spokane, a farmer, a soldier, a nurse,
My mother's work pants, dark brown, her thick bright smile, "Hello, my
 son!"
One in search of a new way because what we have
We all know to be systemic. Unfair. Benefitting just one group on earth.

Men, women, rich, poor, black, white,
Slim build, broken, my brother Jackson's hungry cheek bones, his open
 heart,
People everywhere of every creed and domain
Looking to solve this thorn and hollow

Shock. Dismay. Still too many want to remain the same.
Maybe MLK who gives hope, or Desmond Tutu's Commission,
Maybe Mother Theresa's work or maybe Rosa Park's tired feet,
Maybe none of us really know sacrificial love such as Jesus taught.
That freedom is precious and sweet and giving justice a look
Can bring us home to the doorway I walked through as a boy fighting for
 life,

My shorts with holes in the pockets, my shirt with three buttons instead of six,
My silk brown mouth without water, my stomach wondering where to find a solution for this world.

◊ *After living for many years in this nation of immigrants plagued by a dark cloud of racism and inequality but inspired by those who in my understanding have continued the work of Jesucristo to free the people, I've been moved by the courage and love of many people who refuse to stay silent in the mist of serious attacks to freedom and true democracy, the very foundation of many nations.*

José Hernandez was born and raised in Caracas, Venezuela and has lived in the United States since 1987. He received a Masters of Science and a PhD in Leadership Studies from Gonzaga University. An avid reader of leadership, theology and social issues, José is a quiet activist in conversations over racial injustice and immigration policies related to the developing world. He is the fitness director at Gonzaga University and an independent sports psychology consultant.

WE ARE ALL GOD'S POEMS
Isaiah Hernandez

Put women in a box
And their ideas and sexual freedom
Won't bother powerful men or disapproving eyes in town
So that everything remains as it is supposed to be.

What does "supposed to be" mean?
Put men in a box
And their dominance and power
Can't be contained by targeted women or fearful onlookers in society
So that everything remains as it is supposed to be.

What does "supposed to be" mean?
Put minorities in a box,
Put immigrants in a box,
Put any unpopular category in a box,
And their identity and worth
Won't interfere with the dominant culture or the comfy life of those in denial
So that everything remains as it is supposed to be.

What does "supposed to be" mean?
Put me in a box and my labels and underestimations
Will only spur me on to fulfill my purpose in life and to trust in a God bigger
    than all this mess
So that everything can be as it is supposed to be.
What does "supposed to be" mean to me? Do not be conformed
to this world but be transformed by the renewing.

◊*Inspired by those who have and continue to fight the good fight, and strive for a future of peace, love, and equality for all.*

Isaiah Hernandez is 22 years old and was born and raised in Spokane. He attended Lewis and Clark high school and was a valedictorian. He is a graduate of Whitworth University with a degree in Health Science and a minor in Psychology.

WE ARE ALL GOD'S POEMS
Bridget A. Herrera

We are all God's poems
From beginning, middle, and end
Verses breathed into existence
And shaped into sacred configurations

We are Creator's echoed blueprint
Like tree rings mirrored on our fingerprints
Circles rippling on a still brook as rain drops
Goosebumps on the body read as Braille

We are meter in motion
The swirl of a snail shell
A hair whorl on a newborn's head
Cloud formations twisting into the eye of the storm

We are poems incarnate
Love rhythms broadcasting a drumbeat in the womb
Seeds of life inside the child, inside the mother, inside the grandmother
Like lyrical nesting dolls reciting ancestral lineage for the world to hear

◊*Our tribal teachings tell us there are worlds within worlds. We must strive to see beyond the surface, for when we look deeper, the fractals and repetitive shapes that comprise Creator's sacred geometry are revealed.*

Bridget A. Herrera graduated from Dartmouth College with a Master's degree in 2015. Her focus in the MALS program was creative writing. Delving into the genre of memoir for her master's thesis, *Root Awakenings,* she explored her Caribbean Indigenous roots through an interweaving of landscape, identity, and colonial attitudes that formed her lived experience. She continues to finesse her memoir with the aspiration of future publication. Bridget is an enrolled member of the Higuayagua Taino of the Caribbean where she sits on the Tribal Council. She is an active member of the Community Relations team, and serves as tribal advisor and administrator.

WE ARE ALL GOD'S POEMS
Duane L Herrmann

One God Creator,

one collection of poems:

all colors, varieties and talents –

flower garden created

by Most Great Gardner.

Why? Why are we so many?

So different?

So diverse?

So colorful?

So exciting?

So surprising?

We demonstrate God

is more than we can imagine.

We see so much that we are

and God is even much, much more!

Praise God for our diversity

and expand love to

embrace all that we all are!

◊My influence for the creation of this poem are the many statements in the scriptures of the Baha'i Faith extolling the wonderful variety of the members of the human race as flowers of one garden, leaves of one branch, drops of one sea. My family, as well as many more others, and more all the time, has become a rainbow of colors and I rejoice in our wondrous diversity!

Duane L Herrmann was born and lives on the Kansas prairie. With European and Native ancestry, a citizen of the world, he created a family to reflect that. A member of the Baha'i Faith for over half a century, he finds its message one of hope and courage for the future.

WE ARE ALL GOD'S POEMS
Kimiko Hirota

King's in my Grandma's kitchen.
Wool black blazer leaning against my prom photo,
magnet on the fridge.
Grandma's flipping tortillas on the comal,
a stack already wrapped on the dollar store plastic
covering our wooden table.

Have you ever heard King laugh louder than he preaches?
It echoes against Grandma's teapot collection,
booms over Wolf Blitzer breaking news on cable.
Grandma loves him like she loves everyone.
Yells about Trump, acrylic nails thrashing in the air.
Keeps stirring refried beans between cutting sausage and
dishing plates and frying eggs.

King stares at her. Thinks maybe
she could've started a revolution,
sweat and sugar the ingredients of our Dream.
Her gold crucifix hits against her chest
as she spins to prepare the kitchen
like it's the Last Supper.

King shakes his head. Shakes her hand.
Watches her gather and greet,
Thank and kiss.
He slows at the door
for a moment and says, "I've got to go pray."

◊ *The women who helped raise me are the closest thing to God I've known. My grandmother's unconditional love and grace is effortless, and her nature is worth our daily effort to embody when building a better world. In this poem I thought of Martin Luther King, Jr. meeting my grandma, Estella Armijo Lugo.*

Kimiko Hirota is a poet from Spokane, Washington. Her work has been published in *Voicemail Poems, Railtown Almanac, RiverLit Magazine*, and other anthologies. After graduating from Stanford University in 2020, Kimiko now works for the U.S. House of Representatives Committee on the Judiciary's Subcommittee on Immigration and Citizenship.

WE ARE ALL GOD'S POEMS
Catherine Abbey Hodges

psalming and changing
in The Book of All That Is,
which lies open to every
page at the same time.

And lo! Yesterday's tight bud
has, today, a lip of blue.

The crow has added seven
twigs plus a scrap of foil
to its nest.

You've tinkered
with a rhyme, tried
a different point of view,
reconciled with a friend.

◊*I love the way the poem form challenges us to entertain big ideas with intense economy. In this small poem, I tried to extend the metaphor of the title to suggest the "revisions" of organic, cyclical change as well as active participation in our own ongoing creation and in the making of a more just and gentle shared life.*

Catherine Abbey Hodges' most recent book is *In a Rind of Light* (Stephen F. Austin State University Press 2020). She is the author of two previous full-length collections: *Instead of Sadness,* selected by Dan Gerber as winner of the Barry Spacks Poetry Prize, and *Raft of Days.*

WE ARE ALL GOD'S POEMS
Laura Reece Hogan

When the word came down
that the illiterate should read the molten poems

of creation and recreation, the artisans cast glass
line by lead line, in utterance of cathedral

body. Azure robe of Mary, weeping,
stripped skin of Francis, green of good

Samaritan, bending. Doorways
to heavenly Jerusalem, vivid verse enjambed

in jewel, letters for us, the living
poems spelling ourselves in water, metallic salt,

translucence and stain—not too short or long,
empty in middle space, flat, or falling down

to the crypt, but held in the possessive,
refracting sapphire, ruby, emerald, vibrant orange,

letting it all shine through. Each gaze lifted
intently, open palms catching soft shafts,

a text of becoming,
only fully realized in light.

◊*What came to me was one of my favorite ideas, that we are not only God's creations but also his sub-creators. The medieval effort to catechize the illiterate through images depicted in stained glass windows then came to mind as I thought about how we humans attempt to express the divine through art, even as we are ourselves finite creative expressions of the infinite. I'm thankful for the hope, unity, and joy inherent in this beautiful project.*

Laura Reece Hogan is the author of *Butterfly Nebula* (Nebraska Press) which won the Backwaters Prize in Poetry, *Litany of Flights* (Paraclete Press, 2020), which won the Paraclete Poetry Prize, the chapbook *O Garden-Dweller* (Finishing Line Press), and the nonfiction book *I Live, No Longer I* (Wipf & Stock). She has contributed recently to *EcoTheo Review* and *River Heron Review*.

WE ARE ALL GOD'S POEMS
Jackson Holbert

A boy is writing a letter at his father's desk
in the state capitol. A solitary bulb lights the room.
No one's awake except the mice
the building manager is trying to starve out.

—

The boy will never send the letter it
is to his best friend Grace who is a foot taller than him.
What once might have stood between them now
has moved aside: love, age, fate. They have
entered the stage of their lives
when everything is obscured.

—

But the wind is rising outside the building.
He can hear it moving the limp flags,
rustling the dying leaves from the centuries old trees.
He loves to see the city in the dark, to watch
cars driving through the night. He signs the letter
with his name, his full name. He gets up
and turns off the light and lets his eyes adjust to the dark.

◊While writing this poem I was thinking about personal connection: how the country, the world, is made from two people communicating with each other. And then I thought about how our lives, our thoughts, our hearts are also made from our individual connections with nature. At the end I began to consider how we prioritize our connections with nature and people and how we must, at times, sit and take time to let our eyes adjust to the dark.

Jackson Holbert was born and raised in eastern Washington. His work has appeared in Poetry, The Nation, and Best New Poets. He currently lives in Oakland where he is a Stegner Fellow at Stanford.

WE ARE ALL GOD'S POEMS
Christopher Howell

God, I may be one of your poems, but I think
I resemble more clearly a butterfly-like signal

that wanders dreaming between eons nearly
beyond the reach of even solitude or love.

Or I may be the shadow of one of your eyelashes
fallen at a bend of the garden path along which all

existence journeys, held lightly in your arms. Maybe
I am a shred of the hope that is your basic substance

and our only fuel. My nature aside, surely I am less
than a speck among all of what has, or will, become.

But if I am not a poem, God, in your mercy grant
I may live in the ongoing impulse to write them,

another of your impossibly precious gifts, a small
blossom of which I now humbly offer back to you.

Amen

◊*I confess that I could not seem to get around the title supplied. It is not a title that would have occurred to me, and I felt I had to write directly to it, to find a way to make it mine. I was skeptical, at first, but found that that focus turned the poem into an unusual sort of prayer. And, having said that, I must say also that the poems that have meant most to me have all been a kind of prayer.*

Christopher Howell's twelfth collection of poems, *The Grief of a Happy Life*, was published in 2019 by the University of Washington Press. His work may be found in over forty anthologies, and, recently, in the pages of *Gettysburg Review*, *Poetry International*, *Field*, *Mirimar*, *New Letters*, *Salt*, and *Image*. He teaches in the Master of Fine Arts program at Eastern Washington University, and the low residency program at Eastern Oregon University, and has been director of Lynx House Press since 1975.

WE ARE ALL GOD'S POEMS
Kake Huck

There were wars and rumors of wars among the forms,
for Form itself seemed lost to liberated verse.
Some felt the time had come to fight the flight
from structured truth and nail, and argued
for the strength of their design . . .

"I'm a little haiku
short and stout.
Nature's wisdom
gives me clout."

"Haiku you are not
but frogless nursery rhyme
sinking into pond"

"I'm a lovely young limerick from Derry,
recited last night on the ferry.
The lady agreed
for they both had the need,
and deboarded off to the library."

"Please recall directness is the key.
Only those with focus take the lead.
We can win if we speak bold and true.
Everything straightforward. Let's begin.
Real acronym, real poetry, real win."

"No matter what our form let's come together,
and even welcome in our freest foe.
For ballads, rondeaus, even Flarfy blether,
may brighten minds, encouraging the glow

and lighting of neuronal paths. It's science!
Look it up! Let us not fight but cultivate
each other. There's room for all. Alliance
of all language arts in beauty. We gather
on the page in glory: rondel, sonnet,
triolet, haiku, ghazal, and villanelle;
open form, sestain, sestina, and nonet.
Named for our shape and wisdom, we age well.
When every word is shared from heart to heart,
The rhetoric of love becomes our art.

◊*I was influenced by*
1. *the idea of people as poems*
2. *the thought, "if I were a poem, what kind of poem would I be?"*
3. *my commitment to celebrate my own goofiness in the face of crisis.*
4. *my love of rhyme;*
5. *the President's call to community.*

Kake Huck is a desultory poet and pothead living in Central Oregon. They has (I'm non-binary, not plural) been published in a variety of small periodicals and has two books available by order through your local independent bookstore: *Murderous Glamour: A Novel in Poems*, based on the life of alleged wife-killer Wayne Lonergan, and *Sentenced to Venice*, a collection about the Italian city with each poem just one sentence long.

WE ARE ALL GOD'S POEMS
Brittany Danielle Hunt

God comes to the Woman,
doesn't He?
At wells, in wombs, and tombs
God sticks with them
and lays down stones
My grandmother, she knew God
He was there
in the lilt of her prayer
in the sorrow of her songs
in the aching of her bones
Yes, God comes to the Woman
and to the girl
Men may find God
But God finds me
Of 99, I am 1 to Thee
God comes to Woman
God comes to me

For the man, He parts the sea
Splits the sky
Lights chariots afire
Many a miracle
Does He perform
But a Woman is a miracle
In and of herself
She gives life
Brings light
Heals the broken
Splits open her body for her children
Is scorned, and cursed, and spat upon
Is adored, and revered, and worshipped

Preyed upon and prayed upon
But I don't know
if God is Woman
or man
or none of these
But God is love
and love is Woman
And love is me

◊ *I was inspired to write this poem by a devotional I read that describes the ways men seek God throughout the Bible, but how God comes to women, and meets them where they are.*

Brittany Danielle Hunt is a member of the Lumbee Tribe of North Carolina. She is a graduate of Duke University, UNC-Chapel Hill, and UNC Charlotte and an Instructor at Davidson College.

WE ARE ALL GOD'S POEMS
Drew Jackson

> *Genuine poetry can communicate before it is understood.*
> —T.S. Eliot

We move through this world in verse,
each telling the truth of our own lives,
                yet slant, demanding
that those who approach to read
give no passing glance.

For years I have stood in the mirror, gazing
at this sun-kissed vessel, shaped
from Earth's dust by the hands of heaven, knowing
that the breath of God resides in me, confounded
that so many fail to perceive it.

At times I have declined to receive the message:
I am so perfect so divine so ethereal so surreal,
told to keep my ego in check and
not let it trip over its big-headed self.
But who can call God's artwork a nigger?

I read my skin, my people, our story—
absorb the contours, take it all in.
Every time I return to the words written
in my body there is an unlearning,
a return to my genesis—
my Blackness, in the image of God.

Our work, then:
to pore over each other's lines,

understand why we break where we do,
and not move on until we are moved.

◊As I wrote this poem I was sitting with the biblical imagery of humanity being created in the image of God, Genesis 1:26, Nikki Giovanni's Ego Tripping, as well as these words from T.S. Eliot on genuine poetry. As a Black man, learning to appreciate the poetry of my body and my story has been a lifetime's work, having to wade through and unlearn the messages of our racialized world. I thought to myself, what if we approached each other how we approach a poem—ready to pause, knowing there are more layers than we will see upon first reading, and preparing ourselves to return again and again?

Drew Jackson's debut poetry collection is *God Speaks Through Wombs* (InterVarsity Press, 2021). He resides in New York City with his wife, Genay, and their twin daughters Zora and Suhaila, where he serves as Pastor of Hope East Village. Drew is also the cofounder and President of Pax, an organization committed to equipping the next generation for the work of justice and peacemaking in the world.

WE ARE ALL GOD'S POEMS
VALERIE JACKSON

A white snowflake
Lands on my face
And melts away.

On the distant
Southern horizon
Beneath a layer
Of white clouds

Blue layered on blue,
Snow blanketed mountains
Dream of spring.

Chokecherry branches
Naked of green finery
Reach dry, black arms skyward.

Box elder seed pods
Rustle in the wind.

Puffy chickadees
Take flight
From barbed-wire fence.

Magpies and crows yakety-yak
Arguing over a piece
of white-tail remains.

Longing for Montana
Brings tears
From deep inside me

For my father's cowboy hat
Cocked just so.

Grandfather's dimpled smile
And gentle grey-blue eyes.

Grandmother's deep throated laugh
As she told stories
Seated in her buffalo robe chair.

Mountain Bluebird
Our mother, our matriarch

Has the Mountain Crow in me,
The civilized, book educated
City dweller I am

Left behind old ways
To become only
A shadow of blue rock and cloud?

◊I wrote this poem out of longing for my homeland in Montana. For the mountains and the animals. And for the relatives who remain and those who have passed. My heart belongs in Montana.

Valerie Jackson is from the Apsaalooke Nation (Crow Tribe), Montana. Throughout life, writing, poetry, and song have been woven into the fabric of every experience she has had professionally, personally, and as a volunteer. Writing is a vehicle for catharsis, change, healing and understanding for individuals, families, and communities.

WE ARE ALL GOD'S POEMS
Jennifer James

Yet I pause at the word all.
I don't know if that makes me a pessimist,
A pragmatist, or just a common skeptic.

Perhaps the word all reminds me
Of what the guide said as we
Visited the village near Dachau,
Of how the street, the rooftops, and the heads of
The townspeople were covered with human ash.

Or maybe the word sticks
Because I've seen the glances
In Pretoria when my eight-year-old
White daughter held hands with her
Black friend who was also eight and loved music.
They danced in the former whites-only restaurant
While people spoke Afrikaans with steel in their teeth.

The word stops me
When I think of the twenty-two-year-old
Boy driving eighty in a thirty
Who lost control of his BMW and killed
Four college girls walking together
on a sidewalk at sundown.

My father's father was a monster in darkness,
Drawn to the unholy ruination of his own children.
Should we forgive you, Ellsworth Bennett?

Let God who dwells in thick night speak.

◊*Being married to a genocide and forgiveness researcher, I read his work and wrestle with the problem of evil. Shann and I often talk together about not only darkness but also the natural properties of light. We have come to believe no one can speak for God.*

Jennifer James received a master's degree in counseling psychology from Gonzaga University and currently runs one of the largest global youth sports programs. She has three daughters and has been married for thirty-three years. She loves the poetry of G.M. Hopkins, Maya Angelou, and CooXooEii Black.

WE ARE ALL GOD'S POEMS
Betsy Johnson

and you cannot deny
the ugly.

there's the deep and dim.
the temple wearing tatters.

feverous eyes afraid
of the uninhabitable yonder

and the world embarking into the storm
and terror.

this can all go wrong.
if it isn't handled right.

in the midst,
steadfast be.

do not toss the firmament
to the corner like an old shirt.

praise the leaves that feed on daylight
the flowers that need the dark

to delight
the whims of passersby.

keep the trust
which opens wide the plenty.

care how this ends.

◊My father was an agnostic physician whose rational mind would not allow him to believe in a Greater Than. We would often have intense dinner time discussions, and he taught me to dissect the world and its problems. I realize now that he desperately needed me to remind him of the good and the beautiful.

Betsy Johnson's work has appeared in *Commonweal*, *The Iowa Review* (online), *Prairie Schooner*, *Alaska Quarterly Review*, and *Boulevard*. She lives in Minnesota.

WE ARE ALL GOD'S POEMS
Jonathan Johnson

> "Jews Will Not Replace Us"
> —Neo-Nazi chant

Sure they will. Muslims too.
Mexicans and Central Americans.
Vietnamese. Chinese. Indians.
Ojibwa. Blacks and Africans.
Pacific Islanders. Other white gentiles
for that matter. We'll each be on our way.
And neither winter-bare trees,
nor jobs, nor campus quads, nor neighborhood
porches, nor all-night diners
with their warm porcelain plates
and reassuringly heavy coffee mugs
will remember our names.
And there never was an us to begin with.
Our songs on the radio versus their restaurant smells
wafting down the sidewalks. Never some team,
score, or tribe. Except the all of us someday
to be replaced. The page of each of our poems
to turn. Today, for example,
an approaching constellation,
the young family in coats and gloves and hats,
all five with bright headlamps though
it's only fading gray afternoon.
Only a park. The bouncing, wandering,
glowing points eclipse their faces.
The father gathers snow from a bench,
pitches the snowball deliberately short
of one of his little ones, a provocation
answered with a toss from a comically big,

pink glove at the end of a short, bundled arm.
It's not so bad, being replaced. Watching
from the cold of this picnic shelter
as the young family searchlights its wintry way
down shore and into the woods.

◊*That phrase chanted by Neo-Nazis has been rattling around in my mind the last couple years as an expression of misplaced dread. The most fundamental human us, all mortal people, most certainly will be replaced, and there is freedom and grace to be found in embracing this beautiful inevitability. So it came to me one wintery late afternoon when I saw this young family with headlamps like stars, every distinguishing feature of them invisible except their humanity and bonds of love, which were enough to bring me great spiritual comfort.*

Jonathan Johnson's most recent books are *May Is an Island* (poems) and *The Desk on the Sea* (memoir). He teaches in the MFA program at Eastern Washington University and migrates between Washington; his Lake Superior coastal hometown of Marquette, Michigan; and his ancestral village of Glenelg in the Scottish Highland where his cousins are still crofters.

WE ARE ALL GOD'S POEMS
Cinnamon (Spear) Kills First

Natista
I am holy
I am divine
I am sacred
I am a maker
I am a lifegiver
I am a co-Creator

We are all God's poems.
No that's not quite right
Creator made each of us
Creator is *inside* of us, so
We are all poems and
We are all Gods

In our makings
In our energy
In our poetry
In our being
In our us

My people call Creator
Ma'heo
We teach our children
Ma'heóneve, which means
I am a co-Creator
I am sacred
I am God

Listen
Be still

Sit with it
M a'h e ó n e v e
Can you feel it?

We are all holy beings
We are all sacred gifts
We are all co-Creators
I'm sorry if no one told you
I'm sorry if no one taught you
Especially when you were young.

◊*While drafting a children's book for Scholastic titled "I am Sacred," I was told by a white man that sacredness is a hard concept for children, that they don't understand what it is. I refuted, "Our children know that they are sacred. Yours don't. And that's exactly what is wrong with the world." (The book proposal was not accepted.)*

Cinnamon (Spear) Kills First is a word warrior from the Northern Cheyenne Reservation in Montana. With a Rez education from home, two Ivy League degrees, and an MFA from the Iowa Writers' Workshop, she's a cross-cultural communicator who bridges the gap between Indian Country and the rest of the world.

WE ARE ALL GOD'S POEMS
Chelsey Kirk

In the sway of hips
Saturated by sound and beat
There is a hint
Movement so innate
Responding to old rhythm
Born in bodies before

I live too often suspended
In the midst of many things
Forgetful in the abstraction
Spirits, past and future
Hold us in full attention, waiting
In waves of sunlight along the wall
Near flowers bought just because

Between before and after, presence
Loud testimony to beloved idea so full
It has taken shape
Over and over again
On your head, on hers, here
In the swarm of ladybugs
Flying on the tail of summer

We all quiver and quake
Substance wrapped around mysterious core
Quotidian steps
Stumbling to awaken
The heart recognizing its origin
At night, when the cosmos reveals
Depth and stars fall to be found

◊*As I began my writing process, the title We Are All God's Poems fell into my walking meditation. I realized that I understand this line best through the practice of attention and presence. When my gaze turns to a sky full of stars or my body begins responding to a favorite song, I feel awe and deep comfort in being a part of something bigger and have an innate sense of being deeply loved.*

Chelsey Kirk has written primarily in the non-profit, advertising and storytelling worlds and is honored to be a part of this beautiful project. She teaches yoga and movement classes in Lincoln, Nebraska where she resides with her husband Troy and three amazing kids.

WE ARE ALL GOD'S POEMS
Lynne Knight

One day the body that opened the way for you
to enter the world will be gone, & you'll be alone
wailing as you were at the beginning, stunned

out of warm slow dark into light, inconsolable,
the need to breathe on your own almost beyond
bearing. If you're lucky, you'll no longer be a child,

so you'll know enough to keep your wailing quiet
in the company of others. Maybe at the cremation
or burial you'll cry out, but mostly you'll sit silent,

turning & turning in your grieving as you once turned
in your growing, those slow spins forward & back
while your mother sang to you or whispered stories

about the world that awaited you. If you're lucky.
If your mother could keep you. If she loved you.
From then on, when you hear the word mother,

even if you're a mother yourself, it will mean only
the not-there, the sought-after, the never-to-be.
For a while you'll consider this cruel. Yet

slowly—a different spinning back & forth, back
& forth—you'll hope against all likelihood to see her
again, shining down at you like your first light.

◊*When I think about poetry, I think of my mother, who sang to me when I was a baby, really I think sang me into life because I was a war baby, infected after birth with impetigo in a*

Philadelphia hospital too short-staffed to manage the laundry properly. So for three months, nobody could touch me, except for my mother, who touched me with song—God's work.

Lynne Knight is the author of six full-length poetry collections and six chapbooks. Her work has appeared in many journals and won several awards. In 2018, she became a permanent resident of Canada, where she lives on Vancouver Island.

WE ARE ALL GOD'S POEMS
Elisabeth Kramp

A hum runs through our sound,
proximal and distal to our lexicon's power

to amplify in both feeling and meaning
the sound of our unatomized kind—

theirs, hers, his, and mine, all together
in harmony where inscape dwells deep.

Gentle Breath, breathing in us,
Chemical Catalyst, happening in us,

beyond our caring and our control,
each of us together spells out the word.

◊In writing "We Are All God's Poems" I considered how we are all members of God's lexicon. The "hum runs through our sound" is the Holy Spirit harmonizing with us, helping us see that we're one body and pointing us toward the beatific vision.

Elisabeth Kramp is the editor of *Convivium* and teaches writing at John Paul the Great Catholic University. She and her family live in Southern California.

WE ARE ALL GOD'S POEMS
Stephen Kramp

There's nowhere

        caustic ultramodern sonnet
        in a cheap edition
        creased open on a bench
        out in a garden

  for you

        (more a clump
        of asters really
        with a shaggy
        pomegranate behind
        the plastic bath)

  to go

        now a critical cloud
        thinks your waving lines
        are secretly about
        (and here spots start
        to make you bleed) rain

  but up.

◊*My friends and I used to like to read outside, and a number of poetry books got left out in the elements as a result. This wasn't especially good for the books, but since poems or books can be seen to stand in for their authors, and our ragged gardens did after all need rain, there seemed to be something instructive or meaningful about this particular kind of damage.*

Stephen Kramp is Humanities Chair at John Paul the Great Catholic University in Escondido, California. He lives in the mountains outside San Diego with his family.

WE ARE ALL GOD'S POEMS
Laurie Kutchins

nodding as if we owned
the empire of summer
never a blip on our map
never an eclipse
across our faces
every seed turns
to gold in the blaze
of August and happiest
when reaching for more
more of this vanishing thing
we call the world
creation remind us how
quickly we forget the cry
once labor is over
once birth is finished
how we abandon
fear where it
ripped us open
just to bring forth
a whole field of faces pushed out
of the hot mush
of earth turning
into sunlight
into sunflowers with
seed

◊*What inspired this poem was sunflowers in August -- whole fields of them, and just single stalks. how eager they are to simply be alive and in the world. I felt envy and awe of the sunflowers. At the time I happened to be coming and going from a chemo ward in Minnesota, so I was giving myself permission to project my life force and my desire to live onto the sunflowers. I wanted to be like them -- radiant, healthy, fully here, to have earned my life, and I wanted August to endure along with the sunflowers in late summer. The poem is -- in a sense -- an 'infusion' of sunflowers.*

Laurie Kutchins has three published books of poems and has published widely in numerous periodicals and anthologies. She teaches creative writing at James Madison University in Virginia and has been faculty in summer writers conferences in Taos and Jackson Hole.

DEVADASI: *WE ARE ALL GOD'S POEMS*
Róisín Lally

We are all god's poems, he said.

A thing created.

In the beginning.

The Word.

"Yes," she said,

a poem. How lovely. How true

of goddesses, devadasi, and deeds.

And the word

made flesh.

"Flesh," he said,

flashing fiery eyes

dwelling amongst us

Feasting.

◊*This poem was written in response to the continuous abuse and sexual assault on children in institutions globally.*

Róisín Lally is an Irish philosopher and assistant professor in the Doctoral Program in Leadership Studies at Gonzaga University. She specializes in leadership and ethics, phenomenology, and onto-epistemology. By engaging art and technology, she works to create new methodologies where diverse communities and individuals can grow and thrive and where organizations can nurture an ethically responsible relationship with the environment.

WE ARE ALL GOD'S POEMS
Wendy Wilder Larsen

Usually I hate pigeons.
Rats with wings, we call them,
but today, it's covid-19 time
so everything is upside down.

On my short walk, mask on, head down, I tail
a pigeon feeding ahead of me between the cars.
This one's different— all white, a goddess,
virginal somehow. Alone. no male is strutting
after her. She pecks at the macadam.

She has a set of grey wings on her back,
a design made from her own feathers.
Beautiful, like something woven in a tapestry,
or a spirit symbol in a Navajo rug.

Creeping behind her (she's a she, I know)
I follow her. She moves ahead, I follow.
Desperate, I try to take a picture
to save her somehow— a kind of talisman
to keep hope, to honor her for making beauty
in a dark time. To chime, to shine, to rhyme.

She senses it, stops moving
(posing almost) so I can take the shot.
She knows that double wings are needed
and has made a second set.
I don't think I would have seen this

were it not corona time, nor could I
make this poem, my second set of wings,
to fly my song in this dark time.

◊*After so many days shut up in my apartment in Manhattan, I was taking my daily walk around the blocks, feeling down in the dumps when I saw an almost all white bird with double gray wings across its back. My heart leapt up. I felt hope. I told Chris, the doorman. He agreed she was a good sign and named her "Spirit Bird."*

Wendy Wilder Larsen has two books of poems, *Shallow Graves: Two Women in Vietnam* and *The Gray Whales of Baja*. She lives in New York City and is an avid bird watcher.

WE ARE ALL GOD'S POEMS
Shawn Looks Twice

Sitting in my place in the sun
Face warmed by its rays
I contemplate my life, my journey, its paths
And wonder how it would be written or told

I'd like to think it thoughtfully composed
Artfully crafted and
Carefully constructed
Yet, one evermore in process

At times, it is comprised of lines and lines
With words flowing easily throughout
Eloquent and loquacious
Its understanding clear, as it is fluidly read

At other times, it is jotted prose, succinct
Haphazardly constructed
Pieced together, scrambled and unclear
Completely open to interpretation

Early on, I was forged in the fires of life
Molded by pain, neglect, adversity
Until I was reborn in the waters, the inipi, the circle
Changed, I am now shaped by faith, acceptance, awareness

Unfinished, imperfect, I continue the work, moving forward
There is grace, ease, peace and clarity

Also stumbles, fears, moments of doubt
I've lines yet to be written, my story yet to be told

My life, evermore in process.

◊*My family, and my life, moving forward with lines yet to be written.*

Shawn Looks Twice (Oglala Lakota/Chamorro) was born in South Dakota and raised by her mother and maternal extended family on the Pine Ridge Indian Reservation. She has three children (two grown) and four grandchildren. She currently resides in Surprise, Arizona with her husband (retired military) and their youngest son. Previously in the electrical engineering field, she now teaches at a local elementary school.

WE ARE ALL GOD'S POEMS
AMIT MAJMUDAR

We all want to be joined in holy
metonymy. *You are a part of me*, we want
God to say, *that stands for the whole of me.*
Instead of immanent, just say *man*.
Instead of wishbone, just say *wish*.

Sound out the word, and we are all God's
onomatopoeia. *Gaga* comes from *God mad*:
Coo, coo at the one you love, madman,
across the carousel of the cosmos,
these painted horses circling the sun.

We are all first drafts, shy in public
and rhythmically iffy. We are all
orphan lines yearning to become
couplets, willing to rhyme slant
if that means we don't have to be alone.

We are all written to be read
aloud by the light of a bay window,
out of earshot of the guns and slogans.
Every amnion is an epithalamion,
every kenning is a wedding.

The king of heaven wears a crown of sonnets.
We are all his serifs, we are all winged words,
my sister sestinas, my brother odes.
Don't worry about the ending. We've gotten
an acceptance. He knows us by heart.

◊*This poem takes much of its imagery from the Greek etymology of poetry in poeisis, making. We are made, known, remembered, loved by our Maker just as a poem is by its poet. We are envisioned as our best, impossible selves, too, by that Maker, even though we so often fall short of that Maker's vision.*

Amit Majmudar's latest poetry collection is *What He Did in Solitary* (Knopf, 2020). Ohio's first Poet Laureate, he practices diagnostic radiology in Westerville, Ohio, where he lives with his wife and three children.

WE ARE ALL GOD'S POEMS
M. L. Martinson

A titan, bound to a date palm, wails as his spleen re-forms yet again.

Why all the noise? Yua-Hang—the Jade Emperor, the Pure One, ruler of Heaven, the ancient emanation of Tao itself—yells from the kitchen window. Can't you see some of us have things to do?

What can be more important than my pain? the lonely titan cries out.

My croquembouche, for one! shrieks Yua-Hang. The puffed pastries are so delicate, and my timing with the caramel must be precise or all is lost!

But isn't there more to life than croquembouche, no matter how delectable the pastries and perfectly timed the caramel? the poor titan moans as a sluggish fly inspects the wound.

Well yes, the Jade Emperor concedes, there is Crème Brulé. A well-handled flame is everything.

At this the beleaguered the titan smiles. Yua-Hang smiles in return. Soon the two are planning an eagle pudding.

◊*I'd been working on a collection of satirical gods stories when a friend shared this prompt with me. I have a background in religion and an obsession with Surrealism. This is where the two collided.*

M. L. Martinson teaches literature, writing, humanities, and honors courses at Central Washington University, and his fiction appears in *One Hand Clapping Magazine*, *Crab Creek Review*, and Scablands Books' *Towers and Dungeons* anthology.

WE ARE ALL GOD'S POEMS
Philip Mathew

Poetry in motion
That's what you were
But I couldn't (*wouldn't*) see

You were free verse when I fancied sonnet
A ghazal when I wanted cradlesong
More slam than ballad
Circular in spaces linear

"Why is poetry so difficult to understand?"
Maybe that was my problem
Trying to analyze
when
I should have loved
Looking
when
I should have listened

Is this not Joseph's son?
Isn't his mother's name Mary?
Did not our hearts burn within us
As he spoke to us along the way?

Consider his treasure currently confined
To a muddy pot
Listen to his poems composed
In *starshine and clay*.

◊*The profound theme around which this collection of poems is built challenged me to reflect on the Imago Dei—often hidden, sometimes marred, and frequently blurred by my myopia, but always intrinsically present in each person I encounter. The phrase starshine and clay comes from Lucille Clifton's lovely poem "won't you celebrate with me?"*

Philip Mathew is program director and professor of organizational leadership at Weatherford College. He is the author of *Finding Leo: Servant Leadership as Paradigm, Power, and Possibility* and coeditor of *Global Servant-Leadership: Wisdom, Love, and Legitimate Power in the Age of Chaos*.

WE ARE ALL GOD'S POEMS
Lis McLoughlin

No, We Are not.

Some sing the song of the Goddess
  not of Are, but of becoming.

Others excise the God---
  leaving space for the sacred between All and Poems

Remove the We---
  the ones who learned to cut Nature's web

With We-Are-God out of the way, be left with
All Poems---
  rewilding the page
  resanctifying the universe

Be left, in the end, with All---
  Poems

◊ *As a European-American Pagan, the phrase "We Are All God's Poems" felt counter to, even an anathema to, my beliefs. Yet in writing itself, this poem surprised me with an unexpected Alpha and Omega: it ends the same way the Bible's creation story begins: "In the beginning, was the word."*

Lis McLoughlin holds a BS in Civil Engineering, and a PhD in Science and Technology Studies. She founded NatureCulture (nature-culture.net) through which she directs the Writing the Land project (writingtheland.org). A publisher, editor, and author, Lis lives off-grid in Northfield, Massachusetts and part-time in Montreal, Québec.

WE ARE ALL GOD'S POEMS
BROOKE MCNAMARA

This poem has gained eight pounds
and grown a silver weave through a year
of uncut hair. On New Year's Eve, 2021,
we stayed up till 3am, the boys asleep upstairs,
and like teenagers laughed and chatted
in some delirious, nonsensical paradise,
catching up after months of daily
household tedium. When he asked,
What's your favorite thing about our marriage?
my own answer surprised me:
The grey hair and bellies we're both growing;
it's the most tender privilege to age alongside you.
Dear God, it is not lost on me.
How lucky I am. Dear God,
let there be more lines,
let there be more lines,
and when you've finished this collection,
please place me on the page opposite his.
Close the covers so we can rest
into each other forever, our words merging
in a mixed up gibberish, happy
to be nonsense.

◊*I was completely surprised when this poem emerged; I thought I was going to write about the natural world and the larger scope of humanity. And then a strange form of a love poem for my husband arrived. I realized that in this year of quarantine, our home has been our most immediate habitat, so to write about what's in here is somehow most true.*

Brooke McNamara, MFA, is a poet, teacher, and ordained Zen monk. She has published two books of poems: *Bury the Seed* and *Feed Your Vow*. Brooke has taught at Naropa University in Yoga Studies and CU Boulder in Dance. She lives with her husband and two sons in Boulder, CO.

WE ARE ALL GOD'S POEMS
KEN MEISEL

& the immediacy we seek, when we long for something lost
inside the providence & the radiant chamber of what is holy,
is quite inexact. & it's inexplicable, & it's a disciple to the inscrutable,
& so it's charged & beneficent, & wholly without guile,
she said to me, alongside an old, unused set of train tracks
where the orange grove orchards swelled fragrant with bees
& the noise there, carnivalesque, festive, amounted to
a bewitched summer song. &, you know, she was a military
widow, just thirty, & her husband, overseas, had been
blown up & killed when his right foot grazed a half-buried
land mine still pocketed there, like an angry, kinked little apex god.
& she'd wiggle her delicate neck locket in her hand & open it up,
& she'd display to me his brave picture there, before it
became a twisted memory, just a diffuse light she could feel
more than ever see in the dark, after midnight, while
stirring her tea with two shots of whiskey mixed in it. &, we
were brief lovers &, we were chaperones for one another
as we fell deeper into the scourged unknown &, you know,
hope is an infused aura, she whispered to me: & it's exhaled
in the effluvial mass of all the alive dead – those souls
officiating their theatrical memories, to us. & we are
all god's poems, she admitted & then confessed while
showing me where it was she'd cut her left wrist in the dark
aftermath of his malignant leaving &, you know, when I feel
the scar there, where I cut myself so I could feel & allow his
lofted light in, all I feel is a strange, secured bio-luminescence,
just spectra of his Eros in me. & the whole country, at war,
is a macrobiosis of anabolic life: & it's lively, if we allow
ourselves to feel it. & we become all of god's poems
articulating who it is we'll celebrate when we let a slice
of somebody's deep-lived library of aural noise into us.

& maybe that is the contagion of love: we're osmotic.
& we are all cells in the body politic of lives lived in in us.
& we live it: their spark of life in us to its fullest, oh yes.

◊*This poem was written to underscore the perpetuity existent in those we lose to tragedy and death. In the poem, the speaker both claims her undying holding-love for her deceased husband as well as her noble duty to celebrate the slice of his aural, ongoing internalized life in her. Hope, in this context, is an infused aura; it is the inherited, internalized life force of those we've loved, and lost, and it fires us within a fervent, memorialized spirit. We become caretakers and carriers for the honored dead.*

Ken Meisel is a poet and psychotherapist, a 2012 Kresge Arts Literary Fellow, a Pushcart Prize nominee and the author of eight books of poetry. His most recent collections are *Our Common Souls: New & Selected Poems of Detroit* (Blue Horse Press: 2020) and *Mortal Lullabies* (FutureCycle Press: 2018). He has been published in over 100 literary journals and he donates proceeds of book sales to selected charities.

WE ARE ALL GOD'S POEMS
Maiah A Merino

as I walk through the field
of grass and foxglove
at Nestucca Sanctuary,
the eastern red columbine
invites me into the day
vibrant fire star
offering
delicate blushing petals—
                              nourishment

eaten in dinner's salad
stems and roots poisonous--
returned to the earth.

I was told long ago that often
the thing that hurts and the
thing that heals are
right next to one another

like nettles and bracken fern: side by side
the fern's powder when
rubbed against the skin
                              relieves

what are these
healing agents
we walk past—
missing

like the nettle
used for centuries

in teas and soups
some, would see as dangerous

is it that the Divine design
asks us to look again--
to understand
our layered natures:

                    not evil, dangerous,
                    bad, good, beautiful
                            but whole.

All holy designed.

◊*This poem arrived from my collective memory of Nestucca Sanctuary, a retreat center owned by the Oregon Society of Jesuits, where I spent many days writing and reflecting for about 20 years; it was where I most experienced the Grace of the Divine at play in the everyday, in community and with the land.*

Maiah A Merino, a Chicanx Poet and mixed-genre writer, recently published poems in *In Xóxitl, in cuícatl: Flor y Canto, Antología de poesía*, an international bilingual poetry anthology, is a 2021/2022 Writing the Land Poet and recipient of the 2021 Artist Trust GAP Award. Her work appears in *The Yellow Medicine Review* and *The Raven Chronicles*. As a narrative therapist, Maiah assists others in re-writing their stories.

WE ARE ALL GOD'S POEMS
Philip Metres

all I crave is light & yet
                         the winter
sky is busy   imitating milk
frozen in an inverted bowl

to be a person is a sounding
through,
             host of breath
rehoused & rib scribbled inside

you there above
             the page
casting your gaze over us
wanting us to be your mouth

& what would you say
             with my body
bowed to bear the weight
of a line so taut it sings

& with onward years
drawn to the ground
             lover
who rouses us in the margin

of a dream   guide us to
land we have

>   yet to imagine
> cloud-winged
>   & floating

◊*For twenty years, I have lived in Cleveland, a city with a rough-hewn magic, beautiful autumns, and desperately gray winters. It's easy to lose hope when you don't see the sun for months. But that doesn't stop my reaching.*

Philip Metres has written numerous books, including *Shrapnel Maps*, *Sand Opera*, and *The Sound of Listening*. Awarded fellowships from the Guggenheim and Lannan Foundations, and three Arab American Book Awards, he is professor of English and director of the Peace, Justice, and Human Rights program at John Carroll University.

WE ARE ALL GOD'S POEMS
Pamela Mitchell

She relishes every poem.
She is big. She is Black. She is beautiful.
God cannot contain her joy. Just cannot hold it in.
Therefore, She writes. Details of our color, strength, and beauty
Flourish in her poems

Her poems are blueprints. She sings them first for rhythm, meter and soul.
Then arranges in sometimes balanced, sometimes wild lines.
Then the stories open.

Poems of brokenness. Healed by her love. Sealed with her laughter.
God is a jovial soul. She creates blueprints of brilliant color, gender, species
        and age.
And yes, it is good. Gooey, luscious, delicious, good. Designed to feed one
        another.

All the while She pours her sweet, merciful love over these poems. She
        foresees our mistakes.
We are a garden of flowers within her mysterious mother-mind. God sings
        our names. Convinced of our worthiness. Healer of all wounds. She
        lays her hands upon her poems.

And the words become flesh.

◊ *A memory of one of my patients in NY: a large Black woman, mother of nine children deeply faith-filled, poor, joyful, warm. She shared how she always took time to pray and her children knew not to bother her when she was having her "time with the Lord."*

Pamela Mitchell has responded to the call to nursing (not without argument) for 45 years. She received her MFA from Goddard College, attended seminary at CDPC in Berkeley, returning to the mystery of foot washing. Publications include various journals and anthologies. Her upcoming chapbook is *Finding Lost Pond* by Finishing Line Press. She calls Bend, OR home.

WE ARE ALL GOD'S POEMS
KEYA MITRA LLOYD

Let me confess:
I hoped an N95 might shelter me from your rage,
you from my dark skin.
Turns out you fear me more
when I can't reassure you with my smile.
I didn't know the power of a reflexive grin.
It warded off honks,
the flags you dangle from truck windows like warnings,
like weapons—
I can't remember when I recruited my smile—
or was that you?
Now retired, it climbs out of its fortress.
No longer trained to fear, it stops flinching.
No longer reserved for defense, it roams.
It tries itself out, my smile,
like anything returned to itself does.
No longer at my behest, or yours, it sidles up to me.
Bold and shy, it grazes me with sincerity.
All those years, did I wield my benevolence like a weapon?
Let me confess—
after my mask goes,
I won't be submitting my smile for exhibition.
I want to zip it up inside me
like a seedling I can birth anew
into a world that will not extract from
but smile *for* it.
Help me out, will you?
Let's make this Earth a revelation.

◊ *During the pandemic, I sought peace and connection here in Portland by walking across the St. John's Bridge near my apartment and into Forest Park daily. Oregon has been a sanctuary for me; I've experienced little racism here. Strangely, as I wore my mask on these hikes, I became the target of racial slurs, honks, and aggressive behavior. I began to wonder if some passersby have more trouble humanizing racial minorities when we are wearing masks. This also made me consider if my smile had become something of a defense. This poem is a bid for connection and transcendence.*

Keya Mitra Lloyd is an associate professor of English at Pacific University. Her fiction has appeared in *The Kenyon Review* (2011 & 2015) and many other publications. Keya has completed two novels, a short-story collection, and a memoir. She lived in India for ten months on a Fulbright grant.

WE ARE ALL GOD'S POEMS
Alika Masei

I am from quiet whispers and curious stairs,
from a self-conscious silence.
I am from doubt and dismissal,
but a hunger for change.
I am from a mismatched mosaic
that can never seem
to please everyone.

I am from boxes
made to be broken,
yet reinforced.
I am from tears of joy,
of pain,
of growth.
I am from acceptance.

I am from chlorine-filled pools and wrinkled fingers.
From exhaustion and heavy eyes
as class begins.
I am from "YOU ARE ENOUGH,
but can you push further?"
I am from "sometimes, it's okay to NOT be okay".

I am from the foreign, yet familiar
"Samoan-ness" that is me.
From talo and pua'a at aunty's lu'au.
From my grandfather Mataiau's smile
as we discuss the weather.

I am from the stories of generations before,
their dreams that I may be

unwavering and unapologetic
in my existence.

I am from light,
from love,
from family.

◊This poem stems from my struggles with my sexuality and ethnic-racial identity growing up, as well as how I came to find myself through family. My grandfather Mataiau Masei was a key point of inspiration, not only due to his unconditional love and care for me, but as a reminder to embrace and appreciate the Samoan culture.

Alika Masei is a queer, mixed-Samoan man who strives to build meaningful support for Pacific Islander students interested in attending college. As an aspiring higher education professional, Alika believes postsecondary institutions must intentionally engage families to improve student access and retention, especially for Pacific Islander communities.

WE ARE ALL GOD'S POEMS
Lisa L. Moore

Child next door calls brother brother
Brother doorway sister god

Dog's leap after child's dark ball
Thrown ball gesture of a god

God's filth pain cruelty god's war
These pansies in their dirt their god

Once I held the body of my English setter, too soft and light, as the needle slid beneath her skin. I felt her leaving before her heart had time to stop beating, while her last breath was still in her body. When I think of love, I think of when breath left, the moment I first knew she had really been here.

God in this making beating love
Good dog beating love dog god

Prayer like breath like our own names
Naming breathing making god

◊ *I think of this poem as an interrupted ghazal. A ghazal to embody the repetition, ritual, and practice in spiritual life--a constant turning toward the divine, being knocked away, turning back once again. Interrupted because any practice that is to offer comfort must make space for the abyss of death and loss, the edges that define our experience of this mortal body. Of course, the poem is also a small elegy for a beautiful being who gave me a profound experience of the movement of the soul through the body.*

Lisa L. Moore is the Lambda Award-winning author of *Sister Arts: The Erotics of Lesbian Landscapes*, *Dangerous Intimacies: Toward a Sapphic History of the Novel*, and the poetry chapbook *24 Hours of Men*. She is Archibald A. Hill Professor of English, Professor of Women's and Gender Studies, and Director of the LGBTQ Studies Program at The University of Texas at Austin. Most recently, her poems have appeared in *Zócalo Public Square* and *Waxing and Waning*.

WE ARE ALL GOD'S POEMS
Nima Michael Motahari

Last night I laid on the couch and watched the fire's shadows slowly dance on the ceiling. And thought of my Maman. The anniversary of her death all but a few sunsets away.

My birthdays meant she'd make pots and pots of hot, thick, creamy chocolate for chocolate wafers.

We'd pour the chocolate over yellow wafers smoothing it with the back of spoons. Layer after layer. While she was trying to put them on trays for their passage to the fridge, I'd keep breaking off pieces. Chocolate oozing everywhere, on my hands, arms, on the floor, leaving a trail ending at the fridge door.

And then the times I'd get sick. She'd carry me in her arms through three bus changes, and at least two cab rides, in what always seemed a 100-degree temperature in one of the most polluted cities in the world. On the way back between the three bus changes and the cab rides she'd always stop at a toy store to get me something. We'd get home, she'd put on an apron, and cook for the family.

Some nights when the storm was calling, I'd go to her room. The faint nightlight kept her face barely lit. I'd put my head on her stomach and wrap my arms around her waist. Nowhere would ever be more peaceful.

In the mornings I'd wake up with a pillow in my arms, and the smell of fresh flowers, hot bread, cheese, and tea breezing in from the small dining room. Before my eyes would focus, her hand would gently brush my hair away from my eyes. I'd turn, and there she was with her perfect hair, perfect clothes, and her warm hand on my face. "Did you sleep well little poet?" she'd ask. Yes, I'd nod. "I must've smelled awful last night," she'd remark. "No," I'd reply. "You smell like love."

She'd secretly cry at the misfortunes of others, even those we did not know, words in the back column of the daily paper. And while we barely made ends meet, no one, not even the homeless at the end of the street would ever go hungry. Not on her watch.

All that is bad in me is from the street. All that is good is from her.

◊*I wrote this piece about my grandmother, who I call Maman (French and Persian for Mom). I was raised by my grandparents.*

Nima Michael Motahari was born in Tehran, and educated in England. He now lives in Spokane, Washington.

WE ARE ALL GOD'S POEMS
Melissa Mylchreest

Piecemeal, indelibly, the evening
does its tricks with veils and light:

This is a silver maple. This is a plum tree.
These are the stars coming out. This is the way the body

reconciles what it knows, on patchwork, with leaves
in its hair, in the dark, out of question, out of drought, quietly

and with the fierceness of autumn. This
is kindling, the way fingers and limbs lean

and lock to trap the heat. This is the preface
to a story. Say the plot is sudden, say it's bright

like an agate's hollow, like the fiddle-played grace-note
that turns any song to hymn. Call it a kind of

memory. When you ask what I am most afraid of
and I tell you wasting my life, know that I mean

this. When the neighbor, searching for his
cat, holds us in the quick and blinding

circle of his flashlight, know it is a metaphor
for nothing, but let it play one anyway: the brevity

of hours, our nakedness to the world, our incandescent
laughter. We are nothing in so many ways. You are not

the stars, the evening says, immutable and violently
alive. But we are. There are bones beneath our skin,

and beneath those the numinous and unknown,
scant ingot of something that keeps us burning.

◊ *I don't believe in God; I do believe there is a great deal we struggle to name or explain, and perhaps know only with our animal bodies if we give them license for knowing. This poem is rooted in a very simple experience: Two humans witnessing the last light of day over a small mountain town and ranging widely in the questions that existed in that space. This poem first appeared in* Talking River Review.

Melissa Mylchreest is a writer, potter, and nonprofit director based in Montana. When she's not at her desk or in the studio, you can find her outdoors with her two-legged and four-legged family and friends.

WE ARE ALL GOD'S POEMS
Mary Jane Nealon

Tonight, fire in the hills, the same orange as moon,
        mountain lion burned to the tree he climbed, claws
hold the trunk the way friends hold each other (tight).

Arrival of a breeze that takes smoke, after five weeks
        up and out of the valley, smoke that nearly killed me
in sleep — wake up wake up, I said to myself in suffocation.
        The small dog crying and hitting my arm.

Summer gone, and now, first day of air. Buzz, buzz
        the bees tell me. Under the dog's dish
a flurry of gray slugs crawl like words
        under my skin: weary and misdirected.

In winter I miss the sound of lawn mowers,
        their ability to clip and butcher small sticks,
the smell of the cut, green stains on dog's fur –
        they roll in what they love.

Somewhere else instead of fire, waters rise, men in boats
        hold cats under their coats while in Myanmar

Muslims are slaughtered —

        infrared cameras show their bodies from space.

If I could bear to open my heart to the world

        I would be broken.

◊*In the summer of 2017, my town in Montana was impacted by a series of neighboring wildfires, at the same time numerous other places in the USA suffered extreme floods and in Myanmar Muslims were slaughtered. I wrote this poem in response to the news one night.*

Mary Jane Nealon is a retired nurse and poet. Her memoir *Beautiful Unbroken: One Nurse's Life* was the winner of the Breadloaf Bakeless Prize for nonfiction. She lives in Missoula, Montana.

WE ARE ALL GOD'S POEMS (WE ARE ALL GODS)
MATTHEW NIENOW

and, therefore, at birth an *om*
came pre-rung, like a bell,

whose peal, within our frames,
belongs not even to the ear

in which a thousand-thousand
voices roar in hidden veins,

the forgotten names of those
that made our line, each born

to that hum, each cast
a chance to fight and lose

and love, to live within an
emptiness, and perhaps

then learn how that hollow
hones our sound—

the sound it hurts to make,
the reason we each sing.

◊*I don't believe in god or gods, but I do believe in spirit. I do believe that we are each one small part of a vast collective, bound together in the wild and overwhelming unknown of our Earth — that our lives are subtle, and meaningful, notes in an endless song, sounding mostly beyond our hearing.*

Matthew Nienow is the author of *House of Water* (Alice James, 2016). His poems have been recognized with fellowships from the National Endowment for the

Arts, the Poetry Foundation, and Artist Trust. He lives in Port Townsend, Washington with his wife and two sons.

WE ARE ALL GOD'S POEMS
DAVID OATES

...though like everyone ~~god knows~~ I started as a blue limerick,
yet turned pious after a few revisions and produced
~~in my handsome clever youth,~~ a lovely sonnet
~~five-square~~ pentangular and orotund
~~rich and ripe-rhyming and~~ but with a certain air
of ~~self-~~satisfaction ~~though but~~ too self-enclosed
to stand in this rough world that
seemed to ask for something more – or less –

hard to say what, so many tries, so many ~~draughts~~ drafts
I felt a little tipsy ~~on the way~~ coming home
from the fair, or halfway there, and ~~in the end~~ soon
was pounding out tightly wrought images:
I was god's pot, though poorly ~~throne~~ thrown; I was
a nightingale keatsing in the dark; a ~~twisted thrill of~~
helical metaphysic, a stiff twin of someone
I didn't really know ~~that well~~ at all, a crumpled anger
dropped beneath a Santa Monica barstool
then smoothed out, ~~the~~ next day, and published.

People like a drunk poet. But a ~~perfectly~~ godly one?
Not so much. Turns out we've all emerged
from ~~so~~ many ~~tires~~ tries, and more to come.
Which is, really, where this poem started. A tumble
in the flesh, a fit of ecstasy, a being half spurt ~~and~~ half spirit,
captured and fugitive and ~~all~~ almost free.

◊*I wanted to nudge the prompt towards becoming (instead of static being – God's perfect little poem!). We're a mess, us people, and it doesn't help to pretend otherwise. Flashes of wonderfulness do appear though, and it's our never-ending job to revise, revise, toward that better version.*

David Oates has published two books of poetry including *The Heron Place* (2015 Poetry Award, Swan Scythe Press) and six books of nonfiction, most recently *The Mountains of Paris: How Awe and Wonder Rewrote My Life* (OSU Press 2019). He is general editor of Kelson Books press in Portland, Oregon.

WE ARE ALL GOD'S POEMS
José Olivarez

miracle upon miracle, we were too young—no,
not young, we were too blessed to trace the rivers
back to their origins. my fat & picky brothers & i—
forgive us—we yawned when my mom told us
she had to snap the neck of her first pet chicken
to feed her siblings. pobrecita, amá. we kissed her
cheek to quiet the stories. we wanted to play
video games. we cried when my parents said no
to McDonald's. we never heard all of the yeses
sprinkled over our days. we prayed to god
for everything we didn't have & punched each other
when we weren't given the answers we wanted.
meanwhile, my parents worked in a steel mill,
in a sock factory, at the mall. they snapped
the necks of chickens, so we could savor the stew.

◊*Whenever I start thinking about spirituality, I start thinking about my parents. I want to say that there was and is a spiritual force guiding me forward. And when I trace all of my various blessings, almost all of my blessings trace back to my parents and their love.*

José Olivarez is a poet from Calumet City, Illinois. He is the author of *Citizen Illegal*, has co-hosted the podcast, The Poetry Gods, and won fellowships from Poets House, The Bronx Council On The Arts, The Poetry Foundation, and The Conversation Literary Festival. His work has appeared in *The New York Times*, *The Paris Review*, and elsewhere.

WE ARE ALL GOD'S POEMS
Enid Osborn

implies he crafted us
or perhaps implies
he hears us
our prayers
and the true unutterable
poems of yearning

all my days
I look for signs of love
even as a small child
I studied the lay of sticks in dirt
believing that nothing—not me
not a stick—
was left to carelessness

the stutter of a moth at my ear
the wry tilt of a bird's head
the circling of dragonflies
the pause of a fox on its path
to look me calmly in the eye

I keep myself fit
to catch the gift
to bear it
still I wonder when wild bluebirds
hop along the fence as I—
barely at arm's length—
sweep palm berries from the walk
what possesses them

◊*For some years, I have been delivered signs of love from dear ones and teachers in other realms through enchanted creatures, trees--even insects. Creatures who would normally be frightened off by the presence of a human instead draw near, make eye contact, and interact in ways that can only be interpreted as intentional. The more openly and joyfully I respond to these encounters, the more often they occur.*

Enid Osborn served as Poet Laureate of Santa Barbara, California in 2017-2019. Her book of poems *When the Big Wind Comes* (2015) is set during her childhood in rural Southeast New Mexico. She also co-edited *A Bird Black as the Sun / California Poets on Crows & Ravens* (2011.)

WE ARE ALL GOD'S POEMS
Darlene Pagán

The Virgin on 10th and TV Highway

The boy flies through the intersection
        on a chrome racing bike, the chain link

moustache handle bars set so far forward,
        they appear to drag him down the sidewalk.

The frame sparkles in the same faint blue
        as the Virgin rising in sharp relief

on the mammoth scapular strung over his head
        and flapping against his chest and back.

Stopped at the red light, I watch him dart
        past me into a roiling carpet of fog, until

the bike looks like it's riding on thin air
        and the scapular is really a young girl

in a blue hood, her face pressed to his back,
        arms around his chest, eyes on

the road to make sure the way's clear.

◊*I saw a boy riding a bike on my way to work. Raised Catholic, I had seen scapulars before, but none this large, the size of a poster front and back. My initial fear was that he was going to fall off his bicycle. I'm glad he didn't.*

Darlene Pagán teaches writing and literature at Pacific University in Forest Grove, OR. Her nonfiction and poetry has earned national awards, including Best of the

Net and Pushcart nominations. Her work has appeared in journals such as *Field, Brevity, Hiram Poetry Review, Hawaii Pacific Review,* and many others.

WE ARE ALL GOD'S POEMS
Allison Paul

It's in my nature
to seek place,
to walk through salal,
sword fern, and cedar
and know I'm among kin.

To weave myself
between crags,
cliffs, and canyons that lie
about our divide
and ground us to the divine.

It's a dream to believe in a day
where the chasm closes
and "human nature"
becomes redundant,

where we can enjoy a changed landscape,
like morning alpenglow
painting snow-capped peaks pink,
and revel in the abundance.

◊*This title immediately brought up the theme of interconnectedness for me. It's easy to forget that we, as humans, are nature, despite the ways in which we keep ourselves physically separate from the natural world. This poem seeks to bridge that gap and remind us of that connection.*

Allison Paul grew up in Washington State and spends her spare time exploring the natural world. She is an avid climber, hiker, adventurer, and nature enthusiast. These experiences inform and inspire much of her writing. She holds a Bachelor of Arts degree in Community Psychology.

WE ARE ALL GOD'S POEMS
Emily Pérez

Bay Area Rapid Transit, Oakland to San Francisco, 2019

I find the tattered pages of a madman, poems and plans strewn on a seat,
the sweat, the proteins in the cabin's air setting allergies aloft, the smell
of someone's take-out stacked in cartons wrapped in double plastic bags.
People congregate in hush and hustle, hurtle across a bay and through
a tunnel. More underworld than over. We breathe in an extended in-
between, a wish to be whisked, and safely. Here I have not been for years,
but BART's the same, its unwashed seat covers may contain my DNA,
      packets
of the past, what's passed, the missives of my early 2000's sadness. I studied
vocabulary flashcards here, wanting to pass the test that meant my life
could start fresh somewhere else. On my way to work I shuffled aside.
Strangers ceded space to strangers, nodded into headphones, avoided
one another's gaze. We did not have phones with screens to shield us then,
and while some read books, I read lines on faces, wished those eyes would
      look,
and read me back—
           Outside an AT-AT's born from crane stacks. I'm missing
my kids, the weight of their bodies near mine is the happiest pressure,
the healthiest aperture through which the looking loves. A future I did
not foresee—
          Back then I thought my heartache larger than container
              ships
and just as watertight. Unbreakable. Yearning for a breakthrough. And you?
It's not polite to speak loudly on your cell in here, but social mores say I
      can speak
Across the aisle: Who were you as a child: boy or bone, wolf or merman?
      And did
your scales shimmer? Of course they did. When I was a child I knew God
was hiding everywhere and we might meet on a bus or train. A reason to

> be kind,
to seek the silver seam stitched in my enemies. And yes, I have seen God
in every child, even my own when they are bitter, mean. When does God
> leave?
Or is God still tucked in you and me, tucked also in the man who will
> someday
draw his AR-556 in a Colorado grocery store—is God there, even there—
> patient
in the produce section, when this young man opens fire while tangerines
and pineapples look on, perched like owls full of eyes, awe-full and all
> seeing.

◊*As a child in Sunday school I learned that God could be anywhere, but only as an adult did I understand that meant God was in all people, including me. I wrote this poem between March 15 and March 25, 2021, ten days containing two mass shootings in the US, including one close to home. I wonder if I can regain the grace to see God everywhere.*

Emily Pérez is the author of *House of Sugar, House of Stone* and co-editor of *The Long Devotion: Poets Writing Motherhood*. A CantoMundo fellow and Ledbury Emerging Critic, her poems and reviews have been published in *Copper Nickel*, *Poetry*, *RHINO*, and *The Guardian*.

WE ARE ALL GOD'S POEMS
Robert Eugene Perry

What separates me from you –

Only a thought, a construct
The mind's way of sorting things out
Categorizing according to usefulness
Each entity in its path, desperately
Trying to validate its existence when
Truth is incontrovertible, separation
Unnatural. When I breathe the trees
Agree the sky expands and all
That divides creation falls away
Into the illusion it actually is and
We are all one – the two-legged, four-
Legged, winged and finned, each serving
A divine purpose that cannot be fulfilled
Without one another.

◊*The concept that all living beings are connected has always excited and inspired me. An anthology devoted to that which connects each of us to the larger Life was the perfect impetus to generate this poem.*

Robert Eugene Perry is a native of Massachusetts. His most recent book of poetry *Surrendering to the Path*, was published by Human Error Publishing (2020). As a metaphysical poet, he draws inspiration from nature and endeavors to draw connections between our higher selves and the natural world.

WE ARE ALL GOD'S POEMS
Paulann Petersen

Our sun's one lidless eye. Those gnats
that cloud fallen pears.
The river, a wing sprung
from a mountain's white shoulders—
mantled out, down, lit with glint.
An ocean groaning
her salt-belly, dark with roil.

A hummingbird needle-stitching
our world together bloom by bloom—
fine overcast stitches taken
deep within each flower's throat.

River, ocean, bird, bloom.
Gnat and sun. How can we be
the work of God
unless we are *all* of these?

The wolf who feasts on the warm-blooded world.
That snake whose skin is obsidian mirror.
Stones who are the spittle of stars
making and remaking
a river's slick bed.

These *all* belong.

Every steeple of fir boughs.
Each daylong outlay of cedar-breath.
Each green leaf agog in sunlight.

Mother-silt, father-silt, egg and sperm silt.
The magnolia's labial petals,
unfurled.

All.

◊*This anthology's communal title moves me. A statement, a declaration, it's a succinct and eloquent vision of the sacred universe. "We Are All God's Poems" insists: we humans—even in all our variousness—are merely one part in the family of the natural world. The communal title is, itself, a luminous gift, a gift that gave me my poem.*

Paulann Petersen, Oregon Poet Laureate Emerita, has seven books of poetry, most recently *One Small Sun*, from Salmon Poetry of Ireland. The American Library Association's Booklist calls *One Small Sun* "a veritable master class in the interweaving of metaphor and memory."

WE ARE ALL GOD'S POEMS
ARLENE PLEVIN

There are yellow voices in the kitchen.
Outside the window, all the team captains
whoever picked me last
press noses to the warm glass.
In the distance, a chorus of relatives.

On beige packing boxes they perch,
hopeful as steps.
My uncle swivels and bows--tuxedo tails float
like an apostrophe.
His reckless hands sweep the crowd.
A breath, at once they sing--
recipes for love, for money,
for meatloaf.

The family's oldest sycamore shades them
and the garden.
Fat tomatoes, fatter worms, and grasshoppers,
green as heart-shaped peppers.

Ah, memory, lush garden,
sweet gangster.
We are all poems here.
Yes, there are daffodils, my favorite.
A marsh smell, a golden throat, and wings.

◊*I believe poetry and poems are all around us, in everything (especially domestic) and everyone. I'm especially interested in the poetry of memory, and this poem is a result of that.*

Arlene Plevin is an Emerita professor of English at Olympic College. One of her poems circled Seattle's light rail as part of their Poetry on the Buses program. She was awarded a Fulbright-Nehru grant in India and a Fulbright in Taiwan.

WE ARE ALL GOD'S POEMS
John Poch

The book of James insists on listening.
The book of John is a two-edged sword,
cutting between two realms of the world,
the flesh and spirit, or the bone and the white.
James, John…what is the book of your name
in this Bible of the world we leaf through?
Listen, there is a sword and so much more:

Eating, drinking, buying jackets, the crow
protesting her feet are always shadowed,
barefoot friars, discalced Carmelites,
eels, rock bands called Eels, these are all
the world no matter how they aim at the holy
or every energy adding up to
a current of wind like a river to the sea.

We have our best moments—for one man,
a fox on a fence; or some couple agree,
that one physical kiss in that one film.
While these may be nature's finest intrusions,
they aren't ineffable as words, or numinous.
The voice that makes no sound to say:
In the beginning was the Word.
That is the sword which divides the worlds.
Only, now it moves backward in time.
Watch how it heals a great cut,
a strange eraser closing a wound
like an artist drawing two bodies
together into one.

◊*I think a lot about love, human and divine, one flawed but both holy.*

John Poch's most recent book of poems is *Texases* (WordFarm 2019). His recent book of criticism, coincidentally enough, is called *God's Poems: The Beauty of Poetry and the Christian Imagination* (St. Augustine's Press 2022).

WE ARE ALL GOD'S POEMS
Sylvia Byrne Pollack

Stare into the twin barrels
of a dissecting microscope
peer at translucent opalescent ovals
bobbing in a petri dish of sea water
be patient, focus on the dark spots
inside these eggs until you see
they are the eyes of tiny squid
hatching from the white sacs
one by one   then jetting away

Kneel beside the laboring mare
in a straw-filled stall
stroke her neck   murmur
encouraging words
her body knows what
to do   when to push
watch her lick membranes
off her foal   nudge it
to standing   to suckle

In your own bed
beside your beloved
hold her hand   breathe
with her   through
each contraction
think of possible names
for this new creature
unable to swim or stand
yet perfect in every way

◊*I have been on a bit of an octopus jag lately, watching "My Octopus Teacher" and reading* The Soul of an Octopus. *It took me back to my student days at the Woods Hole Marine Biological Labs where I used to watch baby squid hatch. From that image my mind segued to the miracle of other babies – horses and humans.*

Sylvia Byrne Pollack's work appears in *Floating Bridge Review*, *Crab Creek Review* and *Clover*, among others. A two-time Pushcart nominee, she won the 2013 Mason's Road Literary Award and was a 2019 Jack Straw Writer. Her full-length collection *Risking It* was published by Red Mountain Press (2021).

WE ARE ALL GOD'S POEMS
BERNARD QUETCHENBACH

Who is that flung
in a train coach, or
strapped in a taxiing plane

adrift in a lobby
rapt in forced scrutiny
over an empty phone

or trailing
an English graveyard's
hidden birdsong or

anonymous on a piazza bench
under some bronze
imperial hero?

Pigeons whirl through scattered bread,
clouds shoulder day toward night,
somewhere a violin

plays at a café table, an organ
is heard through the unclosed
door of a minor church.

Who was left behind?
Who slumps to listen
In this other place?

◊ *As the pandemic expanded its reach on the ways in which we interact with other people, I found myself thinking about various kinds of displacement, including that induced by travel, especially solitary travel to unfamiliar places, such as is occasionally necessitated by professional meetings and conferences. Being cut off from much of everyday experience can be disorienting. In the interstices inhabited by overheard music and unfamiliar light, where and what is a "real self"?*

Bernard Quetchenbach teaches at Montana State University Billings. He has published poetry, essays, reviews, and criticism in a range of books, anthologies, and periodicals. With Mary Newell and Sarah Nolan, he edited *Poetics for the More-Than-Human World*, an international anthology of poetry and commentary published in 2021.

WE ARE ALL GOD'S POEMS
Shann Ray

1
My father comes to my room
with a bear skull
encircled by ten claws,
a dark holy
corona unwieldy, uncommon
the glint

of teeth, the maggot-cleaned

2
sheen of bone

and how the tilt of my hand
holds the dead and dying.
His father gave him the dark

holy too. Have you seen

rage in the eyes of another, he asked,

have you shed blood?

3
Then, in the light over the river
my mother's kindness.
Wolf Mountain and Apikuni.
before

5
and we almost see
the outline of their bodies
like gray sphinx below.
All our fathers, Cheyenne,
Czech-German, Lakota,
understood life is made of
death.
My father's old shoulders,
hard

6
brown and brindled
white,
spotted robe
and speckled scarscape
of delivery and receipt, the
sun
he carries and how he
holds
the back of my
head to indicate
what can't be said. God.
Now

7
I kiss the temple above
the cheekbone of each
daughter's holy face

| | walking
Big Timber. | the dark hallway to where
Night fires. | my wife's quiet calls me
Ash smoke dawn. | and when I kiss the
                                     | underside of her wrists,
His father before him | I remember you and am
                                     | free.

    4
with cracked fingers,
a jaw like mountains,
plains, rough lit
skin, long feet set
toward coulees
where mule deer
place their crowns above brush

◊*Listening to my wife recite Layli Long Soldier, e.e. cummings, Natalie Diaz, Wendell Berry, or countless others over me in the darkness of our bed, I think of how each path I've traveled toward love is its own path, some leading down to where I'm lost again, some leading only and ever back to her voice and the joy of her being.*

American Book Award winner Shann Ray teaches leadership and forgiveness studies at Gonzaga University, poetry at Stanford, and poetry for the Center for Contemplative Leadership at Princeton Theological Seminary. His work has been featured in *Poetry, Esquire, McSweeney's, The American Journal of Poetry, Poetry International, Narrative, Prairie Schooner,* and *Salon.* He spent part of his childhood on the Northern Cheyenne reservation in southeast Montana, played professional basketball in the German Bundesliga, and has served as a scholar of genocide and forgiveness studies in Africa, Asia, Europe, and the Americas. Ray is the author of nine books, including *Blood Fire Vapor Smoke.*

WE ARE ALL GOD'S POEMS
Laura Read

I told my class that the reason I love "The Jilting of Granny Weatherall"
is because at the moment of her death,
Jesus doesn't come.
The bridegroom jilts her just like George did
at the actual altar.
Well, of course.
"Digging post holes changes a woman,"
Granny says earlier in the story after her husband
(the one she did eventually have) dies young and leaves her with the farm
and four children, when she's telling us how strong
she was before she even knew she'd also have to die on her own.
I am staring at them with my eyes as large as I can make them to compensate
for the fact that my smile, always there even when I'm saying something
      baffling,
is covered by a mask.
A floral mask to convey my relentless cheerfulness.
Like most children, I was afraid of the dark.
I had a nightlight in my room,
and it had a picture from a children's story but I can't remember which,
it might have been *The Pied Piper*, but that doesn't feel quite right.
I would think I'd remember which story it was because it was my focal point,
the kind they tell you to have when giving birth.
That's a time you have to believe your body can do something
impossible, like going to sleep in a dark room where you don't know
if the objects you saw in the light are staying still or what havoc they might
      be
wreaking and also did you know you could die before you wake
and that the Lord won't take your soul automatically,
you have to ask him to in advance?
One night the nightlight went out and the room spun the way
I would later learn it does when you're drunk.

I must have cried out.
My dad, who was still alive for a few more months, came in with a candle.
Like Wee Willy Winkie!
Who runs through the town! (Upstairs and downstairs in his nightgown!)
He always carried a lantern or one of those candles with a finger loop,
which is what my dad was carrying, though that seems unbelievable
as I'm saying it now. I mean it was the 1970s not the 1870s.
He was not wearing a night cap, but let's put one on him.
Why not? I've heard he had a good sense of humor.
I should have told my class about that night because even if there is no
bridegroom, sometimes a real human being comes in with a candle!
One who is not yet dead!
What I did tell them is that I knew a man who was a priest until he was 50
and then he decided he'd like to fall in love so he left the priesthood
and promptly met a woman to marry.
But then he got lung cancer and coughed through a year and a half.
The first Christmas of his dying, he stayed in our house.
I heard his coughing through the walls.
I felt bad because I didn't particularly like him.
He was friends with my family
and he was always around.
One night we went out to Marie Callendar's, which was amazing
because we never ate out (so many brothers! Throwing bits of pot pie at each
      other!)
and he came with us. Could I please just have a moment
with my mother alone? But he was a kind man. And he didn't get married
and he died at 51 and he did not get to live the life he wanted.
He died standing up at his kitchen sink.
His last word was *Shit*.
I told my class this, and one person laughed, the way you do when you're
      shocked
and you think something is a little bit funny
even though it shouldn't be.
It is. A little bit funny.
I don't know if Jesus was there to meet him.

I don't know why he would come for him after he didn't come for Granny.
I do know it gave me real pleasure to break my students' hearts.
To wield this possibility of nothing. To see their stricken eyes
above their masks. To ask them to watch me sit up in bed
and blow out the damn candle myself.

◊ *Every time I teach Introduction to Literature, I teach "The Jilting of Granny Weatherall" by Katherine Anne Porter--even though I think it might be lost on some of my young students who are perhaps not yet ready to imagine their own deaths as they seem such a long way off. But I've been thinking about death all my life, since my father died when I was six. I love that this story asks us to imagine what dying might feel like by bringing us into Granny's stream-of-consciousness. It makes me feel like I'm practicing.*

Laura Read is the author of *Dresses from the Old Country* (BOA, 2018), *Instructions for My Mother's Funeral* (University of Pittsburgh Press, 2012), and *The Chewbacca on Hollywood Boulevard Reminds Me of You* (Floating Bridge Press, 2011). She served as poet laureate for Spokane, Washington from 2015-17 and teaches at Spokane Falls Community College.

WE ARE ALL GOD'S POEMS
Carlos Reyes

—for JR Lovell, at 9

When you step onto
the huge table top stump,

when you walk around
growth rings only with your eyes

are you going down
or rising with the contours

to the mountain top?
The giant fir was felled,

history loaded up.
carted away, what

do you make of the mystery
of all that, what is it you see?

When your footsteps
lead you around and around

between dry and wet seasons
summer and winter—hard winters

what do you make of it all
as you, a tree grow taller?

◊*As my nine-year-old grandchild and I were walking, we came upon a large stump. She noticed the concentric rings and we got to talking what they represent. Later that day I got to thinking about our excursion and wrote this poem.*

Carlos Reyes travels widely and his poetry reflects that. He is the author of 11 volumes of verse. Recent poetry: *Sea Smoke to Ashes* (2020), *Two People in the Night Along a River* (2019), *Along the Flaggy Shore, Poems from West Clare* (2018), *Guilt in Our Pockets, Poems from South India* (2017), *Pomegranate. Sister of the Heart* (2012). Forthcoming: *Wrestling the Mistral* (2021) and *Osage Elegy* (2021). Recent translations: *Poemas de amor y locura/Poems of Love and Madness, Selected Translations* (2013), *Sign of the Crow*, Ignacio Ruiz Pérez (2011). Prose memoir: *The Keys to the Cottage, Stories from the West of Ireland* (2015). He lives in Portland, Oregon when not traveling.

WE ARE ALL GOD'S POEMS
Dr. Susana Reyes

My Beloved
I have loved you for all eternity.
I released you in that moment
to the earth and its ruggedness

full of energy and ready for the journey,
the lily where life started, my mother's voice in which all
is okay, all is possible and soft spoken.
When you felt lost,
you were in fact found.
When you cried out to me,
I cried out to you.
When your soul wandered,
I wandered through the walls of your adobe casita
beautiful the way we ate together with bliss
our spirits full of my sisters' smiles our brothers'
faces adorning us with kindness.
When you caught glimpses of me
in the hummingbird's valence and the wing
of Nayarit in San Pedro Lagunillas in my casita
where happiness played outside and created
our childhood, remembering now we are one and
never alone even when you cried in agony, feeling abandoned.
We remembered then our Luna Girl, sweet, smooth as she meditates,
her head on my lap the whole universe I am peace
knowing I would come seek you and whisper
I am that I am when you turned toward me the greatest of these,
when the eyes of your heart caught mine, I who caught you

appeared in your life again with the fogón and Abuela
carrying herself as one whose hands created all,
the longing became the reunion, the knowing that separation was not.

◊*I live my life knowing the great Source of all, God, lives in and through me. As is the nature of being human, it is easy to lose track of the Presence, and the reunions that I'm blessed with evoke words of wonderment and awe that, often times, result in a dialogue of sorts with the One. It fills my soul and brings me back to that zero point or stillness where I am that I am shows me his face….in my heart. As the words flow, I write. And, I save them to return to in moments that can be described as dry spells or "dark nights of the soul." I feel blessed that I am gifted with the words. This poem contains some of those words.*

Dr. Susana Reyes is an education administrator, currently the Assistant Superintendent of Operations for the Pasco School District. Along with family time, she enjoys running, reading, and writing in her spare time.

WE ARE ALL GOD'S POEMS
Susan Rich

In the beginning, no one did their assigned tasks.
When God was supposed to create different genders

they found themselves staring into an inland waterway
wondering how many droplets could slide over a stone

in a moment. God was like that, she lived for riddles.
She'd calculate a finite number of compounds, hydrogen

copycatting twerk moves and oxygen two-stepping up-close.
Who knew water could be so malleable? Neither male nor female—

without color, or, more honestly, infinite colors iridescing.
No one asked water if it came from a rib; did it know a certain serpent?

God kept opalescent eyes on the covalent bonds, deconstructing
the anatomy of water which seemed a slippery notion at best,

like the idea of designing and drywalling the world in seven days.
Who would believe it! God hummed a little as molecules

kept growing and so did all genders, their hair like waterfalls.
Somewhere God read a billion seconds would take 32 years to count…

They napped then; stretched their neck like a house cat
or perhaps a Tyrannosaurus Rex. And what about cloud genders?

A bank, a billow, a scape? How much water might God transition in
via communal faucet, lake effect, favorite swimming hole—

◊*My piece began with the idea of a questioning female God and soon the poem wanted to go further, to not be limited by a specific gender. I suspect that sense of humor is also a characteristic that might be helpful.*

Susan Rich is the author of six books of poetry including Blue Atlas, from Red Hen Press (2024) and two anthologies including, Demystifying the Manuscript: Creating a Book of Poems (2023) with Kelli Russell Agodon. Her work appears in the *Harvard Review, O Magazine,* and *World Literature Today.* She is a recipient of awards from the Academy of American Poets, Artists Trust, and the Fulbright Foundation. Susan lives and writes in Seattle.

WE ARE ALL GOD'S POEMS
Debra Rienstra

and some of us are drab
little things with fierce names

enfolded in the ordinary duff.
Bushwhack through meadows, set out

a net of light, and what may appear? A moth,
perhaps, like this papery scrap

tossed up in a cache of winged
secrets, royally mantled, fringed

and furred with umber-siena-sable
designs as if, after this—look closely—

what could possibly be
more worthy of your gaze?

All it takes is the patience to turn
our shadows inside out. We share

an alphabet of atoms, at any moment
poised to scatter and gather, yield up,

transform. Seed to leaf, leaf to breath.
Even decay is only temporary dis-

integration toward some shimmering
new coalescence. We strive to close the gap,

kern the space between each utterance
at once ephemeral and everlasting.

Arrayed, all of us, like one of these,
our beauty in the ardor of our yearning

as we are lured into light.

◊*I came across a story in National Geographic about a nature photographer who, unable to travel during the pandemic, decided to photograph insects near his home for the Photo Ark project. He happened upon a specimen of the long-toothed dart moth (Dichagyris longidens), a creature never before photographed in the wild and rarely seen at all. I could not stop staring at the photo— such beautiful detail on such a tiny thing—and I wondered what other mesmerizing mysteries we overlook.*

Debra Rienstra is professor of English at Calvin University in Grand Rapids, Michigan, where she teaches early British literature and creative writing. She is currently working on a book of nonfiction essays on faith and climate change (forthcoming with Fortress Press).

WE ARE ALL GOD'S POEMS
Katrina Roberts

He braved the wind to skate my sled a river's reach
so I could see eels pulled up from holes in ice.
That I might cup small hands to quench my thirst, he
hiked me down the whole meander of rocks to Lion's Head Spring.

He showed me dip, and catch, the controlled grace of slide
before lift, to square and feather oars, so I'd row myself ashore.
He told me not to "write my name," to hold a tiller still, to inscribe
a steady line across the crumpling page of sea. He checked locks,
battened for storms, banked fires to keep me warm.

Twice, I saw him cry. More? When a child, I could so easily lie
draped atop his length, my ear against his sweatered chest, though
I must not move an inch, he ordered, so he could rest.
A wound watch, the startling engine of his heart
drubbed my headbone, a tuning-fork set ringing by the bird
caught within his ribs. That yellow wool pressed ridges in my cheek
and yet, was soft.

Now, as two pills loom like icebergs in the center of a spoon
of applesauce brought to his lips, his clouded eyes
slide through the room's chill to find mine, and I swallow hard.

◊*Embodied, we're both burdened and blessed. We're all states of matter, elemental, shaped by the grounding, gestures, and generosities of others. This poem tries to honor the source of song, the inevitable pain of consequence and transformation, the beauty of fortune that brings us together even for a brief moment, on this planet, in this galaxy.*

Katrina Roberts has written books including *Underdog, Friendly Fire, How Late Desire Looks*, and *The Quick*, and edited an anthology. Her graphic work appears widely;

her manuscript *Likeness* was finalist for the Pleiades Press Visual Poetry Series 2019. She teaches and curates the reading series at Whitman College.

WE ARE ALL GOD'S POEMS
Dave Rock

The second best night of God's life was when God met God in a crowded room and without words almost understood. Shyly fed small talk to the furnace smile. Held hands going home, unbearably struck by the touch. Undressed shaking, lifetimes feeling ugly inside almost washing away in body fluids, shared breath, light. God rocked God in arms until almost felt enough, and came at the same time as God.

The first best night of God's life was 9 months later, when God fell from between God's bloody legs and again took first breath. God swore to God that God was a fucking miracle. Wired the fuses through flooding with God. Felt so safe in God's arms.

Learned to crawl, walk, touch the edges. Learned that God burned, was broken, not allowed. That God would not always come when God cried out. Felt loved one moment for being something, hated for the same the next. Became ashamed of face. Still felt safe in arms, most of the time.

God told God shut the fuck up, don't be stupid, there's something wrong with you. Learned God wasn't God. Had to struggle and fake it to be enough, to maybe be beloved. Decided everything was bullshit. Got ripped at the gym. Dressed slutty. Said Yes without knowing wanting. Said No with buried longing. Pretended not to give a fuck. Bought better stuff, then better stuff. Sometimes felt almost safe in arms.

Sat in judgment over God's singing voice, entrepreneurial spirit, body, children, God. Watched God declare the tragic necessity of war on God. Voted, protested, argued, wept. Hated God for Hating God. Killed God for killing God. Pressed buttons, ate, watched things, slept. Killed, was killed, cheered at killing, forgot about killing, screamed at killing. Pressed buttons, ate, watched things, slept. Felt never safe in arms, sometimes.

One day saw across crowded rooms instantly and almost understood. Could love any, be with any, all was. Just wanted to hold so, remember, ugly fresh washed faces. Didn't want to own, save, use to feel. Just to cross the space between without permission, without need. Stayed in the doorway watching paralysed whirlwind what believed what had to be in order to.

Just wanted to make feel safe feel beautiful.

From across rooms, from doorways, saw hair fall across necks, felt hands raise glasses, heard breath appear.

◊*This poem came from the heartache of how easy, and how hard, it can be to see grace and the sacred in others, both human and non-human, from the experience of love and grief that comes in those moments when my senses are suddenly completely awake and I can see everything is itself, everyone themselves, and the hunger to remember to treat all life as 'holy,' whatever holy means.*

Dave Rock is a writer and spoken word-storyteller based in Ireland's West. His work has appeared in various international journals and he has read and performed very widely across Ireland, the UK and parts of Europe. He also teaches transformational creativity workshops.

WE ARE ALL GOD'S POEMS
Lex Runciman

Houses, cars, families, portraits, mistakes, a dime each,
> dozen a dollar in an antique shop – old photos

passed by, though I think of one of them now, quick look:
> shaky focus, no colors, a line of dark hair

under a canvas cap tipped back, and a forehead – only that.
> Ancestry a mystery, Black, or Native, Guatemalan, Irish …

does this matter how we care? As for the face not pictured,
> eyes unlined perhaps – easy and composed.

Or elderly, welled with tears, or bright with creases smiling.
> For sure I hope other palms and fingers touched that skin,

enjoyed the feel of it – such touch allowed, such touch
> encouraged. As for the mouth unseen,

what can we say beyond anger, desire, thanks, and song?
> We are all God's poems. We'd need to listen.

◊*As the poem suggests, an antique shop within a few blocks of where I live features a washtub of miscellaneous photos, most of them black and whites, each of them anonymous and quite partial representations of lives lived. This poem looks at – I want to say 'focuses on' – one such photo, to suggest that imagination can be empathy.*

Lex Runciman has published six books of poems, including *The Admirations*, which won the Oregon Book Award. His selected poems, *Salt Moons*, was published by Salmon Poetry in 2016. A new volume, *Unlooked For*, is his most recent publication, also from Salmon Poetry in their 40th year of publication.

WE ARE ALL GOD'S POEMS
Tania Runyan

But not the one he scrawled on a meter ticket during open mic
so he could clomp on stage at 8:57 to impress the girl

or the late-night, tortured rose-petal lines scattering the pages
of his comp book as he squinted through the window for a star.

We aren't even the perfect canzone chiseled and shining
in the incandescent workshop light. No, we are more perfect

than that: words unrolling from his sunlit temple as he props his feet
on the bow of the kayak, cicadas electrifying the trees.

He's a poet full of beauty but not overcome by it, lungs in flower,
just one bright stream of coffee quickening his pen.

He stares straight down the side of the starboard
to the bottom of the pond, where algae wave their wispy arms

and the glass ladders of diatoms tumble in the silt.
All reaching, all invisible. We are more than his creation

but the way he speaks of it: loveable as a dog's ear twitching
in a dream; beautiful as an old woman laughing, pretending to cup

the wolf moon in her mitten; wrenching as a war vet diving
at the sound of a balloon. We are all his poems,

daily sheafs of them written, stacked, and bound with the wild ivy
he doesn't have the heart to stop, submitted

simultaneously to the water and wind, the merciful earth,
his own heart that publishes everything that comes across its desk.

◊*The best poems come from focus and freedom working together to create a writing state much like Csíkszentmihályi's flow. I thought about some of the scenarios in which I've been able to attain this state (which doesn't happen all that often), then imagined God writing all the poems of us from that perfect flow—a state of utter love, playfulness, intelligence, and joy.*

Tania Runyan is the author of the poetry collections *What Will Soon Take Place, Second Sky, A Thousand Vessels,* and *Simple Weight*. Her guides *How to Read a Poem* and *How to Write a Poem* are used in classrooms across the country. She received an NEA fellowship in 2011.

WE ARE ALL GOD'S POEMS
Penelope Scambly Schott

The broken daughter, her spine
misshaping her fragile back

the old dog, dragging his lameness
partway into the yard

the rose bush, mostly flattened
by the town garbage truck

The rose blooming come springtime,
the daughter shaping words on paper,
the dog, old dog, tonguing my hand

◊*My daughter has had medical problems, I was remembering my old dog, and a contractor just smashed my rose bush. I hope it does bloom this spring.*

Penelope Scambly Schott is a past recipient of the Oregon Book Award for Poetry. Her newest book is *On Dufur Hill*.

WE ARE ALL GOD'S POEMS:
Luci Shaw

Hope That Glimmers

The absurdity of a world
on its knees, whose fingers, even,
may be traitors and whose breath
may breed death. Its command:
Stay away, this is the ultimate act
of friendship.

Like the light at the bottom
of the well, hope shines small,
but if we stay alert, head over edge,
we may watch the water shimmer
with possibilities.

At noon, a pale sun.
How to begin to heal, believing
the world will not die, but lives on
for us to tell the stories
to our grandchildren?

◊ *A lovely invitation resulted in this new poem.*

Luci Shaw is a poet and essayist, and since 1986 she has been Writer in Residence at Regent College, Vancouver. Author of over thirty-nine books of poetry and creative non-fiction, her writing has appeared in numerous literary and religious journals and in 2013 she received the 10th annual Denise Levertov Award for Creative Writing from Seattle Pacific University. Her newest collection, *Angels Everywhere* (2021), appears with Paraclete Press.

WE ARE ALL GOD'S POEMS
Katy Shedlock

recited live
in a dark and crowded cosmos
flowing freely at the bar,
ice and glass clink,
spirits stronger in the shadows.
Whatever whirling chaos
in the background
fades to formless
when the divine face
hovers over the mic.
Let there be you
and me alight
with attention,
three minutes
not an eternity
but eternally
alive in each
other's memory.
All beloved poems
eventually get read
at funerals, our lives
summed in a few
short lines. What
are we, but spoken
Word, easily chilled
by the cold void?
And it was so
good, anyway,
the warm cloud
of breath lingering,
vapor and steam

float briefly
then drop
let's return
not to dust
but to the dark.
We listen
so much better there.

◊*This poem is influenced by the language of Genesis and the loss of performance poetry during the pandemic.*

Katy Shedlock is a Methodist pastor and slam poet in Spokane, WA, where she received an MFA in poetry from Eastern Washington University

WE ARE ALL GOD'S POEMS
Derek Sheffield

How we all are is what I am
trying to write about, but the chickens
with their chicken racket make me open their coop
into the backyard where they become orange-eyed T-Rexes.

Back in my chair and how we all are
is a rattling buzz from across the room.
Jeez Louise! I think, and get up to silence my phone
and, for good measure, twist the blinds down.

I take up my pen and paper,
and the tickle on the back of my neck turns out
to be a sugar ant now on my finger
being carried to the door and blown into a spring day.
Look out for the chickens, I say. We are all,

and out of nowhere, my cousin like a flood,
our whole lives like brothers, like when he taught me
how to drive in his Mustang while cranking
"King of Pain," and a thousand other things.
I'm smiling, not quite alone in this room, remembering
how angry and stubborn he was, trying to stay silent
to keep me from once again ordering the same thing as him—
the restaurant's bustle, our fathers and the waitress waiting.
A waffle with strawberries and whipped cream, please,
even though I never liked waffles. All our lives,
like how we walked each other across the fields
and through our fathers' silences. God
is what they were always taking us to church
to learn about but I always had him.
And here we are, four years since his son

came out and I clicked Love, and he's once again
keeping his words to himself.
He's not a bad man. He's a good one. The best man
at my wedding and I at his. His name is Neil.
I get down on my knees and bow into his silence.

◊ *This is a poem of process. The process of making it and the process of living what has gone into it. And it is a poem of pain and open arms and hope.*

Derek Sheffield's collection, *Not for Luck*, was selected by Mark Doty for the Wheelbarrow Books Poetry Prize. His other books include *Through the Second Skin* and *Dear America: Letters of Hope, Habitat, Defiance, and Democracy*. Sheffield lives on the eastern slopes of the Cascade Range in Washington and is the poetry editor of *Terrain.org*.

WE ARE ALL GOD'S POEMS
MARTHA SILANO

and we are all magnificent like the tail of a fox
and we are all the nothingness after a white dwarf dies out
and we are all the stiff wind and the slack the stubborn and the stickpin

we are all god's eaglets even when we feel itchy
in a blue taffeta dress even when we walk toward a hollow
where a river otter roamed but the hollow is filled with beige homes that all
        look alike

we are all god's goodness like a glassy lake a few ripples
a kingfisher in a bare tree we say goodbye to the goldenrod in the fall
to the bleeding hearts in the spring, welcome the poppies the color of egg
        yolk

as the goldfinches molt from brown to lemon we are lemons
in a front yard in Tampa the wonder of citrus and sumptuous situations
like the president's dog is a rescue dog from Delaware poisoned as a puppy

we are that pup grown up and padding around the White House
his food bowl full of pure food and we are the crystals inside the snow
and we are the tea leaves at the bottom of the cup we are god's teacup

the leaves when we read them say HOPE
and we are the firewood stacked by the house enough for a long winter
some leftover for the termites and the beetles for the long summer that will
        follow

and we are the whispering but we are also the screams and tears
and oh wows of those ladies who watched their sorority sister's swearing in
our bones are bits of stars bits of explosions we explode like spent suns like
        suns

planets dying and being born and we are the heron that lost its way
landed in the middle of a busy street in Manhattan on a little patch of grass
between 8th and 9th Avenues, a little stunned but figuring out where to find
    the fish

and when we are not fishing we are dancing to Prince & the Revolution
The Beach Boys or Snoop Dogg or Janell Monae we are chillaxing to the
    chill beats
because we are god's playbook of starlings and pill bugs and meteors some of
    us living under

a mossy roof some where monsoons soak adobe brick
because when we care for the sick because when we take the chaos
and turn it into a kiss because when we work toward solutions we are a
    bombshell

of success because when we live like we're a string quartet
we belong to god and god belongs to us as we scotch tape the hate
to the love till the love sticks and the hate finds another planet where it can
    thrive.

◊ *I want to express my gratitude to Kelli Russell Agodon, who provided me with my own personal writing prompt to draft this poem, and to Danez Smith for their poem "my president," a key source of inspiration.*

Martha Silano has authored five poetry books, most recently *Gravity Assist*. She is co-author of *The Daily Poet: Day-by-Day Prompts for Your Writing Practice*. Her poems have appeared in *Poetry*, *American Poetry Review*, the *Best American Poetry* series, and elsewhere. Martha teaches at Bellevue College and Hugo House in Seattle, WA.

WE ARE ALL GOD'S POEMS
Esperanza

In this dark, silent room,
seeing stars, a screen
of constellations calcified,
the film of my dark universe,
I find beauty.

In this dark, silent room,
my breast colonized
by doctors' needles
piercing my flesh,
I nod when they say,
"This won't hurt."

In this dark, silent room,
I get lost in the eyes of the nurse
holding my hand,
squeeze when it hurts.
I know she can't save me.

In this dark, silent room,
I discover deposits of calcium,
suspicious, irregular shapes
clustered like grapes on the vine.

In this dark, silent room,
my words, like lines in a poem,
erase, replaced by the language
of Chiron and love poems
written by God.

◊*In this poem, I describe my thoughts and feelings during a biopsy. This wild and unsettling experience made me think about our humanness, our mortality, and the beauty in others and in our world. I felt deep gratitude.*

Esperanza's poems have appeared in *Blackbird*, *The Gettysburg Review*, *The Kenyon Review*, and other journals. Honors include poetry fellowships for the *Gettysburg Review's* and *The Kenyon Review's* conferences. Assistant Director of Bread Loaf in Sicily and co-coordinator of the Lorca Prize, her poetry book, *Esperanza and Hope*, was published in 2018 (Sheep Meadow Press).

WE ARE ALL GOD'S POEMS
Donna Spruijt-Metz

God, YOUR desk is vast
        —and since YOU are
                everywhere—the desk is
                      —in some sense—
                          portable—
                          like the stars

I imagine YOU hitching up
        YOUR glorious robes—
                YOUR living garment
                      gathering it all up—
                      to sit

at YOUR desk—
        cluttered
                with notes and fragments—YOU
                      are diligent—YOU show up
                          to the blank
                          space

every day, and today [if YOU
        have things
                like days]—well, let's call it
                      'today'
                      —or 'now'—

YOU are working
        from a prompt—it's
                endearing—all around YOU
                      [which is everywhere]
                      are scattered

    tiny sparks of light—
        YOUR rough drafts
            waiting for release—longing
                for each other—and maybe a place
                    at YOUR side
                    [which is everywhere]

◊*What pulled me towards the poem that emerged was Luria' story, part of Kabbalah, which tells how God placed sparks of diving light in holy (but fragile) vessels, and how the vessels shattered— how they weren't strong enough to hold the sparks. It became our job to repair the world by gathering together the sparks of divine light through being kind, by doing good. Thinking of the idea that each of us—imperfect vessels--contain a spark of divine light, is what unfurled into this poem.*

Donna Spruijt-Metz is Professor of Psychology at the University of Southern California. Her first career was as a classical flutist. Her poetry has appeared in venues such as the *Los Angeles Review*, *Copper Nickel*, *RHINO*, *Cortland Review*, and *Poetry Northwest*. Her chapbook, *Slippery Surfaces* was published by Finishing Line Press.

WE ARE ALL GOD'S POEMS
Kim Stafford

I say thank you to my ghosts by living,
by waking, by being afraid behind my mask,
thank you to the woman who delivers flour and oil,
to the bird spirits where I scatter seed, to the nephew
who calls to tell me he is so far down he doubts I can
ever find him, and thank you to the truck driver night
running north from fields to my door with potatoes
I split open like broken hearts to find my brother's
reasons for departure thirty years ago today, my
most intimate ghost who missed his chance to
forgive himself by being gone. Brother, be my
ghost for guidance when I'm lost to beckon
with a fallen leaf surrendered into lace.

◊*I was reading Jericho Brown's poem "Say Thank You Say I'm Sorry" when I realized my late brother, who took his life in 1988, has thereby missed these many years of war and terror, and how I remain here to represent his spirit. As I walked, a late leaf fell from a tree, and I realized it was a message from my brother to me.*

Kim Stafford writes, teaches, and travels to restore the human spirit. He is the author of a dozen books, including *Singer Come from Afar*. He has taught writing in Scotland, Italy, Mexico, and Bhutan. In May 2018 he was named Oregon's 9th Poet Laureate by Governor Kate Brown.

WE ARE ALL GOD'S POEMS
John Struloeff

Here we are in this season of pausing, delays, and cancellations,
   in this strange new weather that has, with its invisible powers,
changed all traffic somehow, people walking in streets
   that used to be filled with cars, our playgrounds and schools emptied,
yellow tape telling us to stay away, police lines blocking intersections,
   arrows guiding our ways down empty corridors.
We've read about this in books, about times of plague and revolution,
   seen it in historical films and speculative fantasies,
but now it's our world, the only world we have.
   Who would have thought that sitting alone at my desk each day,
in the corner of my quiet living room, my new workspace,
   listening to that lone car whisking past on the empty street,
would be so stressful? Sitting behind the glass looking out
   at the blue sky of August, watching a neighbor cross the parking lot
to her car and vanish.

                         But here I am – and you are, too,
whoever you might be, so far from each other – feeling the withering weight
   of this viral weather, our needs un-paused, our bills still arriving,
our children still growing too quickly behind this cold, unfair fishbowl
   glass they face each day. We all know it must start again –
the old un-paused world of connection, the un-social-distanced celebrations
   –
   and so we continue our solitary existences in the face of it,
holding out hope as we cook our old meals that are somehow
   strange now, hope that we can gather beside one another,
to hear the poetry in the voices of old friends and distant family,
   see each other's smiles un-masked again – not the Zoom smiles,
but the actual smiles we remember, the laughs we remember

from before this time of pause and distance. To *un-pause.*

A few months from now, perhaps. God help us, another year.

I'll see you then. Our un-paused selves.

◊ *I remembered sitting at the window by my desk one day during the early months of the pandemic, looking out at the strangely silent world -- a world normally bustling with cars and people -- and saw a woman wearing a mask rush across the nearly empty parking lot, get in her car, and race away. The situation -- this new pandemic existence -- struck me as surreal, and I felt the depth of my isolation behind that glass.*

John Struloeff is the author of *The Man I Was Supposed to Be* and *The Work of a Genius*, with individual poems in *The Atlantic, The Sun, Prairie Schooner,* and elsewhere. A former Stegner and NEA Fellow, he now directs the creative writing program at Pepperdine University.

WE ARE ALL GOD'S POEMS
Melanie Rae Thon

i was thinking
  about the bees

down deep in the flowers
  of the trumpet vine

how there were three
  in one blossom

drunk & dazed & none
  was sorry

because orange flowers
  are whole worlds

& there was enough
  for all
    & more
      & plenty

& anyway nothing
    on earth
  is meant
    for one alone

which is why the bee
  has no word
    for love

the thing that is all
       & ever

◊*I am sending along my bees. Hope. All we can know, ever, ever. With Love & more.*

Melanie Rae Thon is a recipient of a Guggenheim Memorial Foundation Fellowship, a Whiting Award, two fellowships from the National Endowment for the Arts, and a Lannan Foundation Writer's Residency. Her most recent books include *As If Fire Could Hide Us*; *The Voice of the River*; and *Silence & Song*.

WE ARE ALL GOD'S POEMS
Russell Thorburn

Even the foam churning on the shore
in its whale splashes before returning

to the deep water, the massive desire
for an inward roaring, can't take away

this wonder of being alive. At the cliff
we hear the sibilant waves

on this wintry day come crashing
down in a drunken breath,

and accept we are one with loneliness,
one with a below-zero chill that bites.

Ten feet from the grave of Charley Kawbawgam
we brush the lines from our eyes,

stamp our feet to bring back blood
to our toes, and think of his roots

here on Presque Isle, where he lived
with his wife Charlotte and fished every day;

when he laid his ear to the earth
it trembled for the Chippewa man

and his auricula grew large, as if his ear
were able to hear everything.

Now Charley walks along fallen trees,
rock almost bleeding,

and hears Lake Superior dreaming
with strange wide eyes.

◊*This poem comes from the spirit of Lake Superior, Mother Superior to some, who heals birdwatchers, long walkers, swimmers, and paddlers. My son and I recorded its waves this winter, looping ten minutes into four hours, for a meditation upon the power of nature and how it nurtures us when we are in pain.*

Russell Thorburn is the author of *Somewhere We'll Leave the World*, published by Wayne State University Press, which draws on the poet's own experiences while imagining fictional characters and personal heroes. He has received numerous grants, including a National Endowment for the Arts Fellowship and Michigan Council for Arts and Cultural Affairs. He was an artist-in-residence at the National Mojave Preserve where his poetry was featured in an exhibition at the Kelso Depot Museum. His new one-act play, *Gimme Shelter*, is set in a bomb shelter during the mid-sixties and the Cold War apocalypse. He was the first poet laureate of the Upper Peninsula.

WE ARE ALL GOD'S POEMS
Janelle Timber-Jones

If we took time
If we went deep
Into the Soul of who we are
Who or what might we find?

The soft little animal I am
The Song of 100,000
Ancestors
Loving me into existence
So that I might be
An expression
Of their beauty

◊My love of reading and writing (poetry and prose) has been a healing balm.

Janelle Timber-Jones (Northern Cheyenne) has been in personal recovery for 37 years. The Earth and Stars have guided her. She believes that renaissance of truth in history, through the generations, needs to be nurtured in us all.

WE ARE ALL GOD'S POEMS
Rosemerry Wahtola Trommer

I want to read the poem of you—
want to hold in my breath
your intimate rhythms
want to translate in my lungs
the silences between your stanzas,
want to feel in my heart
the sharp tug of your turns,
the communion of your inner rhymes.

I want to follow
the ever-emerging form of you,
want to know which words
are appearing even now
in the divine cursive
that writes us all,
want to wander in your ambiguities,
wonder about your secrets,
marvel at your beauty,
be wrestled by your oppositions.

I want to recite your lines
again and again and again
so your stories
are the allusions that inspire
the emerging poem of me.

This is the poem in which I admit
every poem has the potential
to break open the heart—
imagine the size of the book.
This is the poem in which I remember
the heart was made to break open.

◊*I was thinking of how reading poems out loud and learning them "by heart" changes everything about the way that I read them—makes the experience and my understanding of them more profound—and how if we could learn by heart the poems of each other and carry them with us, how deeply that would change the way I move through the world. And from a writing perspective, I love how the form emerges—ever surprising—and that inspired this poem, too.*

Rosemerry Wahtola Trommer is the co-host of the poetry series Stubborn Praise and co-founder of Secret Agents of Change. Her poems have been featured on *A Prairie Home Companion, American Life in Poetry, PBS Newshour* and *Oprah Magazine*. Her most recent book, *Hush*, won the Halcyon Prize. One-word mantra: Adjust.

WE ARE ALL GOD'S POEMS: *CHASE*
Seth Brady Tucker

> *If the world hate you, ye know that it hated me before it hated you*
> *- John 15:18*

The pages of scripture thin as
the skin on an onion, the lord
hovering over with love or hate

        depending on whom you ask;
        your god has gone from warm
        as summer concrete to cold

as deep winter lakes when you are
taught that Psalms guides us to ostracize
the sinner, to abandon them. You race

        to find selected scripture, a chase
        through furious wrinkled pages, each
        folded to find the words easily, a race

with no prizes. You know that the bible
has the word love written in it more
than four hundred times; hate more
than two hundred; you know poetry is powered

        by repetition. You know where to find nearly
        any scripture by memory, each instance of the Lord
        speaking marked in green, love in blue, hate in red,

Your seminary teacher is a lovely woman
& so terrified of both sin & the sinner that hate
is our morning search. You press your palm down

> on her favorite scripture, refuse to play, you want
> to ask her, *how is it that all these weak men & weak*
> *scholars turning our love to fear, our charity to greed?*

You understand the temptation to scribble new laws
between these old translations of man, manifest fresh
good words: make love the only summons for our gods,

love as refrain, love as replacement, love as prayer?

◊*The central image of the poem comes from my time in seminary school, which is a required bible-study class for Mormon kids, and is an early memory of the first time I truly began to reframe and question my own conception of scripture and God. Ultimately, it was the true deep reading and memorization of scripture that caused me to wrestle with the very human failings and questionable intent of the writers and translators of the word of god and how those small and large edits can be used to control and manipulate.*

Seth Brady Tucker is executive director of the Longleaf Writers' Conference and he teaches creative writing to engineers at the Colorado School of Mines near Denver. He is senior prose editor for the *Tupelo Quarterly Review* and is originally from Wyoming. His work recently appeared in the *Los Angeles Review, Driftwood, Copper Nickel, Birmingham Poetry Review,* and others.

WE ARE ALL GOD'S POEMS
BRIAN TURNER

There will be rain in the story.
A series of voices. Birds. Maybe
a character flaw some find charming.
There will be pain, of course,
and laughter. Some small
sweet gesture, like the way
you used to hold my face
in the soft cups of your palms
before kissing me, moments
we gather into something
one might call a life. This
story we tell ourselves
as loved ones cross over
one by one.
              We are learning
how to care for the dead, each
in our own way. So, too, the living.
We lean our heads back and listen
to music translated from the air
as memory draws our fingers
through a loved one's hair
before brushing the stone
to reveal the pooling shadows
of the chisel.
             With each day's
passing—I am learning how to speak
with the dead. With you. It's something

like prayer, I think, the way others might
talk to god within the vaulted spaces
of the body, one's voice spoken
into the long corridors swept clean
of shadow, there by the opened windows
where the birds might one day
fly in at dawn, singing.

◊If you look up Ilyse Kusnetz (and I hope you do), you'll find that she's an incredible poet and that her life has been given a temporal frame of parenthesis, as historians and gravestones do: (1966-2016). But I can feel her presence in our home, in my life, in my body. There is grief in this, and there is love. I am attempting a kind of conversation, a kind of prayer. This poem is part of that.

Brian Turner has written a memoir, *My Life as a Foreign Country*, and two collections of poetry, *Here, Bullet* and *Phantom Noise*. He's the editor of *The Kiss* and co-edited *The Strangest of Theatres*. He directs the MFA at Sierra Nevada University.

WE ARE ALL GOD'S POEMS: FRONTERAS
Patricia Valdés

She,
la niña mestiza, knows borders…was born in one "con Los Estados Unidos"
the one, some say, is "una herida abierta… an open wound"…
she knows borders… the ebb and flow of the cultures, of English and Spanish…
the place where she witnessed the ripping of families, the laceration of the bodies
…the joy and the strength of love when borders were crossed.

She,
la niña mestiza, wrapped herself in the jungle, discovering an unknowable void,
so familiar, so foreign to her, she, the tactile girl… she heard, in the future, how mother Theresa
"listens to God and God says nothing, and she says nothing, and God just listens."
She, la niña, heard the silent cadence of poems that… God and Coatlicue and her ancient Gods
whispered in the silence as they listen, not in English, not in Spanish
…she listened in a silence she came to know.

She,
la mujer mestiza, went "al otro lado…al Norte" where she "flowed" between cultures,
in isolation, she bore witness at a pandemic time of pain, death and a cacophony of hatred of the others;
others, who should be kept out by a wall - a border wall.
Others… like her.
She bore witness at a time when border crossing seemed impossible;
when border crossing, could have helped them survive.

She,
la mujer - the woman, sat in isolation; crossing borders through a phone,
bearing witness to the grief of others.
She listened to the sound of aloneness,
to the piercing pain of a ninety-year-old veteran.
He too crossed borders, remembered poems for his sweetheart,
letters of undying love in a faraway time.
His quiet tears loudly crossed the space where they were held by la mujer,
... North American man y la Mestiza.
They traversed borderlands of culture, language, age;
of the earth and the heavens,
where he believes his sweetheart holds his love poems.
A place where no form is needed,
where in the silence, he, and his God's love, forever hold her.

She,
la abuela - the grandmother, heard the whisper
of her five-year-old granddaughter:
"Abuela, do you know there is an invisible thread that connects us to God?
You can cross through …it is easiest when you bring me to the forest."
She wondered how we could weave invisible threads;
threads that cross borders - fronteras.

◊*At a time of a pandemic, I sought refuge in those who came before me, in the philosophers, activists, poets, painters, musicians; those who have brought light into this world. I wrapped myself in the silence; in the love of God. Through this piece, I attempted to give voice to the love stories, resilience, interconnections and hope that allows us to not only survive but thrive.*

Patricia Valdés spent her childhood in Mexico, she made a home in Spokane where she raised her children, and now delights in her grandchildren, family, friends and community. She served as a therapist in the community, she worked as an administrator and taught at EWU, and currently serves as a bereavement counselor at Hospice of Spokane. She writes poems about social justice.

WE ARE ALL GOD'S POEMS
Angie Trudell Vasquez

When you pray
to the silver maple
arms across its bark body
cheek against grizzled wood.

When you drink
from the water faucet
lined up after recess
your friend's lips
pursed in glory,
clear stream bubbles
between flesh and chrome
sunlight highlights
brown hair, small limbs.

When you dance
at a summer festival
the band cues a holy drum roll
a sax bellows blue grass blankets
winter toes relish spring,
green blades tickle ankles.

When you breathe
the scent of cinnamon
candy your papa bought
to cover tobacco breath, coffee
the scent of wet wool warms the spine.

When you let the mother of four go ahead
take back the cart for a stranger,
when you pick up park litter the critters

left behind, stretch for the high pieces
caught in evergreen boughs.

When you brake for a squirrel,
release the mother raccoon with her babies
in a forest glen outside the city
where creeks run and rivers pour fish
where oak roots mingle spread gossip
beneath our hiking boots, our footprints.

◊ *This poem was inspired by thinking of all the ways we can embody God's teachings through our everyday actions, and Joy Harjo's eagle poem. I like to think of people as poems anyway, so it was a good exercise.*

Angie Trudell Vasquez is the current city of Madison Poet Laureate. She received her MFA in poetry from the Institute of American Indian Arts. Her third collection of poetry, *In Light, Always Light*, a finalist for the New Women's Voices Series, was published by Finishing Line Press in 2019.

WE ARE ALL GOD'S POEMS
Jeremy Voigt

a cento from GM Hopkins' notebooks (pp 144; 508; 509; 534)

The villain shepherds
and misguided
flock—Ah! flock!

how my thoughts
move towards my shame,
my shame
blazoned in shame's own
color blood.

But such a lovely
damasking in the sky
as today I never felt before.

Found some daffodils wild
but fading. You see
the squareness
of the scaping well when
you have
several in your hand.

The brow was crowned
with burning clear
of silver light
which surrounds the sun,

then the sun itself
leapt out with long
bright spits of beams.

◊*I am a poet and teacher, currently working on a PhD thesis reading the poems and notebooks of Gerard Manley Hopkins ecologically. I have fallen in love with Hopkins' notebooks, and find his voice in them terribly hopeful. He might be known for the "sonnets of despair" but he was a poet/person/priest capable of tremendous hope and joy. His love of the natural world and of people inspire me. Reading him closely is making me a better poet and a better person. I have been making found poems out of his notebooks. This is one.*

Jeremy Voigt's poems have appeared in Prairie Schooner, Nimrod, Gulf Coast, Post Road, Willow Springs, BPJ, and other magazines. He has been nominated for a Pushcart Prize, and was runner up for the 2019 Discovery Poetry Prize. His manuscript has been a semi-finalist or finalist for the Dorset Prize, The Crab Orchard first book prize, the Brittingham and Felix Pollak Prizes, 42 mile, Marsh Hawk book prize, and the Miller Williams prize. He lives by a large lake in western Washington.

WE ARE ALL GOD'S POEMS
Ellen Waterston

Pretend you're an envelope with a note inside written
in the form of a prayer. The all of you, your em—
dash laugh, your run-on mistakes, is the orison
penned by the Poet in an elegant metaphysical hand,
then folded and placed inside the envelope that is you,
and gently mailed into the world when you are born.

Your devotion is written within the within of you.
The infinite space between each you-word is where
heaven abides. Petitioning a distant deity is an unnecessary
use of time as the gift of light is everywhere, the palace
of love and Nature is within you! Prayer is but a reporting,
a telling, a circadian celebration of your imperfect perfection.

Every day, if you can, turn more and more inside out
so the you-prayer is nurtured by more and more light.

◊*This poem, which I have been chasing for a while, is an effort to reiterate how sacred each of us is just as we are. The challenge is to nurture, to care for that uniqueness in the face of all that life delivers. Thanks to the inspiration provided by this anthology I have had the opportunity to revisit, rework and, hopefully, improve the inside out-ness this poem tries to capture.*

Ellen Waterston is the author of four poetry and three nonfiction titles. *Walking the High Desert* (University of Washington Press) is her most recent nonfiction. She is founder of the Writing Ranch and the Waterston Desert Writing Prize. She is on the faculty of the OSU Cascades low-residency MFA program.

WE ARE ALL GOD'S POEMS
Amerra Webster

In the winter my people pray and sing for snow.
We pray for snow to come and settle and rest in our homes.
We pray for snow to grow and grow and grow on the peaks
of our mountains and the uneven grounds of our valleys.
We pray for the sky to open up and for kʷĺncutn to bless us
with the white flurries of hope and medicine we need to
to heal. This year, we pray more than ever for snow knowing
that if we don't, this year may be the last year that we and the ones
we love are given the transcendent opportunity to pray for
good health and healing.

We pray for the frozen earth that holds the snow up, the earth
that tells the snow to absorb the pain and sicknesses we knew
all too well over the past year. We pray for the cold winds that
comfort and keep our precious snow in its sacred form. We
stand in awe of the love that the snow and the wind have for each other.

When the cold winds are no longer strong enough, we feel the
earth begin to warm and soften; we mourn the old. Who knew letting
go of pain could hurt so much? What keeps us going is the promise
of the warm rays of sun that touch our lands and that slowly begins to melt
the snow and allow for its divine transformation to water; the water
that will rinse away the accumulated pain and sadness we knew over the
last year.

It softens and gives into the natural process of release and forges
trickling paths into the soon to be unfrozen earth under it.
It's a seemingly gentle but ferocious process to witness.

Have you ever seen your sicknesses wash away and return
deep into the earth ready to be reformed and healed?
Has kʷĺncutn ever put your pain and sorrow away?

As our sicknesses roll down the mountain, our songs also return
to their resting places. They are tired but never weakened from helping
us bring good health and medicine to our families and people.
They seek rest and go to bed, knowing that next year we will call
them down again to help us put away the sicknesses we have yet to
      experience.

We know our songs and past year's sicknesses are fully gone when frost no
      longer
accumulates in the night; when the mountains turn from a sea of
white to a rolling body of green and blue; when the sun kisses us early
in the morning. We are healed, we are strong, we are ready for the
inevitable sicknesses and hardships we will face when our
sacred snow melts and until it is called back when we need it again.

◊ *Every year my people pray for snow to come and wash away our sicknesses and help us begin our new year in a good way. This year, these prayers have become even more important as the world experiences the COVID-19 pandemic. While many of us are all dealing with mounting feelings of uncertainty and sadness as a result of the pandemic, what remains certain and consistent is that our wintertime prayers of good health and healing have not and will never stop.*

Amerra Webster is a Séliš u Qĺispé sm?em (Salish and Pend d'Oreille woman) who is from and works on the Flathead Indian Reservation in northwest Montana. Amerra is defined by her roles as a daughter, granddaughter, niece, aunt, partner, and friend.

WE ARE ALL GOD'S POEMS
Ellen Welcker

> *...to want nothing, to ask for nothing, but simply to sort out your own mind.*
> *—Olga Tokarczuk*

My crone hair is flowing & my petty little wounds all my stagnant inner bogs
     my wet & unlit fuse   my metals are heavy   as a hog with human face   & I'm all made up
 of marks   like a sack of skittish hares I'm out here wan & pinkish
     barking at the wind
  in the blazing manzanitas   plucking goose from skin & gawking, often softened
by a river-facing folding chair— I'm out here   in the whiteout & I'm whining
     yes

I am
     often softened by the children's never-
ending hair, my hand attempts   a sectioning, an ordering of air   I
am googling home haircuts &   possible owls,   bewildered apologizing
    talking power ballads   &   cradling   my empathy   like a tiny saw whet who coos   at the women
    idling in their cars
     the rest stops full up with them the pull-outs packed & none of them   not any looking up   at Jupiter   they are me
    I am they
 & our empathy   is out here too, somewhere: see, I can laugh
    I am ashamed
        I am
   I am.

◊*Bewilderment is at the root of my practice and my way of being in the world—I have written before that "I know / the world prefers me / bewildered" and this not-knowing feels like the only way I am able to approach titling a poem in this way! What a great challenge. I humbly submit I know nothing, and still I am awed to be here.*

Ellen Welcker's books include *Ram Hands* (Scablands Books, 2016) and *The Botanical Garden* (Astrophil Press, 2010) and several chapbooks, including "The Pink Tablet" (Fact-Simile Editions, 2018). She lives in Spokane, WA.

WE ARE ALL GOD'S POEMS
Michael Dylan Welch

we are all God's poems—
the hermit crab
that scurries away
from the anemone
closing at my touch

sunlit wildflowers—
we are all God's poems
in the meadow
stretching to the glacier
on the mountaintop

sand in the lee
of a fallen gazelle—
we are all God's poems
in the last light
of the desert sunset

wheat waving
under storm clouds
as the harvester passes by—
we are all God's poems,
even prairie deer mice

Douglas fir
and towering pines
swaying over us
on our last summer hike—
we are all God's poems

◊This tanka sequence progresses through different biomes offering a variety of plants and animals as God's creatures, and thus as God's poets. The movement of the title line to a different position in each verse may suggest the ongoing procession of life.

Michael Dylan Welch is founder of the Tanka Society of America and National Haiku Writing Month and is president of the Redmond Association of Spokenword.

WE ARE ALL GOD'S POEMS
Leslie Williams

Picking up the packet

of radish seeds

some little hairs grew

longer on my arms

◊*I'm always interested in hope. I was prompted to write this poem as a way of articulating the radical thrill of feeling the interconnectedness of God's creation in one's own incarnational way.*

Leslie Williams is the author of two prize-winning poetry collections, most recently *Even the Dark*. Her work has appeared in *Image, The Christian Century, Poetry, America,* and elsewhere. She is also a Godly Play teacher and in training to become a Spiritual Director.

WE ARE ALL GOD'S POEMS
Paul Willis

What is it about an open-sided canopy
that seems both airy and complete?
This one is broad and white on top

with inner billows of purple fabric
asterisked by darkened stars.
We feel a little like royalty here,

the setting sun making us all luminous
as we trade poems and noble comments.
Breezes blow through long-needled pines

beside us, and mourning doves
coo their refrain. We sail together
like Antony and Cleopatra in silken barges

on the Nile, like Aladdin on his carpet,
and who knows when or where
we will land? As Robin Hood lay

dying in an upstairs chamber,
he shot an arrow out the window
that has yet to come to earth.

◊*During Covid, we conducted classes out-of-doors under large tent canopies scattered around our California campus. This was a marked inconvenience for the technologically minded, but lately look back and see it was a chance to connect with words and one another in a new and better way. Plein air!*

Paul Willis has published six collections, the most recent of which are *Little Rhymes for Lowly Plants* (White Violet Press, 2019) and *Deer at Twilight: Poems from the North*

Cascades (Stephen F. Austin State University Press, 2018). He is a professor of English at Westmont College in Santa Barbara, California.

WE ARE ALL GOD'S POEMS
Diana Woodcock

In Uganda, I saw poverty,
corruption, inequality,
acid-burn victims I refused to turn
my face away from.

But then again, I saw the Grey-
crowned cranes, Marabou storks –
those keepers of the dumpsters,
and Cinnamon-chested bee-eaters,
African Golden-breasted buntings,
the Variable Sunbird. And I heard

the Black-chested Snake-eagle
cry out from its regal perch atop
the tallest pine. And when that darling
of a bird, the Superb starling
with its iridescent body of turquoise
and royal blue came to feast on the lawn
of my run-down hotel, I knew

this was a country I could love,
forgiving its sins. And when
the sound of frogs in the swamp
below my window took up their chant
every dusk, I knelt and kissed Uganda's
soggy ground. Rainy season just
beginning, mosquito larvae hatching,
pure waters like goddesses to ripen
the grain. Let it rain

and wash away all greed and evil deeds,
pour over Uganda pure splendor.
But what did I know of the country's
sadness? At the church on Sunday
I thought, How lovely so many young people
in the pews. That was before I knew
people from fifty were counting the years
till sixty.❧ I sought refuge

along the Victoria Nile—Murchison
Falls where The African Queen was filmed,
1951. Where rhinos no longer roam.
I saw hippos and buffalos,
crocodiles with their sly smiles,
waterbucks and elephants,
giraffes and hartebeests.

And so many birds in a place
human residents had to evacuate
1907 to 1912—Tsetse flies spreading
sleeping sickness throughout the riverine
woodland, savanna with its acacia trees
and Borassus palms, the Nile Delta.

I should have stayed, never coming
in out of the rain. Insane, you say,
giving my heart away
to a country of such poverty,
corruption, inequality.

But that crocodile along the Nile,
idling its life away, and the birds:
Shoebill stork, Malachite kingfisher,
Goliath heron, Grey-crowned crane,
and that delicate African jacana

tiptoeing over water lilies,
walking like Jesus on water.

❧Average life expectancy is 58.5 years.

◊*This poem is about a recent experience in Uganda, where I went to conduct research on birds, but in the process fell in love with the country and its people.*

Diana Woodcock is the author of seven chapbooks and three poetry collections, most recently *Tread Softly* (FutureCycle Press, 2018) and *Near the Arctic Circle* (Tiger's Eye Press, 2018). She is the author of *Facing Aridity* (a finalist for the 2020 Prism Prize for Climate Literature, Homebound Publications) and Holy *Sparks* (Paraclete Press). Recipient of the 2011 Vernice Quebodeaux Pathways Poetry Prize for Women for her debut collection, Swaying on the Elephant's Shoulders, she teaches in Qatar at Virginia Commonwealth University's branch campus.

WE ARE ALL GOD'S POEMS
DIANE YOUNG

We are stardust brought to life, then empowered by the universe to figure itself out
      And so we emerge from starfield

Our lives are like islands in the sea [that] hang together through the ocean's bottom
                                      and sea.

      Archipelagos of scintillant poems
      rising from the cosmic sea that sings us up
      out of its emptiness, we
      salt the waves that break against us having ridden
      the depths amongst us to erode us into our singular forms
      that we might drift stardust back toward the deep
      as waves pull us back, atom by atom, into the sea,
There are more atoms in your body than there are stars in the entire Universe
      into emptiness we emerge from to return to, to bear into being for awhile.
If you lost all your empty atomic space, your body would fit into a cube less than 1/500th of a centimeter on each side. Neutron stars are made up of matter that has undergone exactly this kind of compression
      Motes of stars in a god's eye, capable of spectrometry, we
      scan what sings within the atom's empty margins
      where the lines of an interlining life begin and end,
      our selfing scribing itself in a double-helixing script
      that organizes the stuff suspended in the emptiness of atoms
      into a living lattice to make a poem of embodied space—
           mind and brain dreaming in the verse of the skull
           heart and lungs measuring the stanza of a ribcage
           blood birthed in the porous marrow of the quatrain of bone
           singing its way through chambers
           and arteries and veins and the capillaries
           that surface in deltas to the feed the cell-thin sea of skin

> that marks out from in,
> > that breathing membrane that keeps us whole—

Every time you breathe in, you're breathing atoms of air that were once inside another human being

> inhale

Right now, if you take a deep breath and then exhale, by the time a year goes by, approximately one atom from that breath will wind up in every other person of Earth's lungs at any moment in time

> exhale, inhale

We have approximately one atom in our body from every breath that every human has ever taken

> exhale

> > —where, from our emptinesses, through our transpirations,
>
> we write endlessly
> > > the couplet that never quite closes
> > > the sonnet (oh, argument for love!) that each we are

Notes:
First quotation: Neil DeGrasse Tyson, *Astrophysics for People in a Hurry*
Second: William James, "Confidences of a Psychical Researcher"
Third: Ethan Siegel, "How Many Atoms Do We Have in Common With One Another?"
Fourth: Brian Clegg, "Twenty Amazing Facts About the Human Body"
Fifth, Sixth, Seventh: Ethan Siegel, "How Many Atoms Do We Have in Common With One Another?"

◊I've been studying Buddhism and practicing meditation regularly for the last few years and have found the shift from the "original sin" paradigm in which I was raised by parents who never really took the hellfire and damnation part very seriously to the "basic goodness" paradigm of Tibetan Buddhism very heartening and encouraging (en-courage-ing). Emptiness as a spaciousness that accommodates arising and the full expression of energies (i.e. beings) influenced this poem—as did the principles of interbeing and interdependent arising. I'm also an avid reader of lay science, especially systems theory, astronomy, and anything of the interesting factoid variety

that resonates with interbeing, interdependence, emergence out of complex systems (including emptiness).

A poet who's practiced in universities and public schools, while throwing stock and waiting tables, Diane Young is currently hammering out poems while working the gig economy as a teacher. Everywhere she's been has taught her to believe in language and sudden beauty to transform the heart and thereby move the world.

WE ARE ALL GOD'S POEMS (*FANTASY IN A TIME OF CHAOS*)

MARLY YOUMANS

Splash across the drift of dreams,
Fly to promised island peace,
Weave a nest from golden gleams
And curl against its sunny fleece…
Hear the music of the spheres
Sighing with the weight of years,
And, star-like, know
What it means to flame and glow.

There you'll glitter, night or day,
Not a soul to know your light,
Freed from those who hunt for prey,
Saved from mortal fears and blight,
Roar of war and press of tears,
Bonfire vanities and fears,
Your sunshine beams
Spilled in hid but ceaseless streams.

◊ *"Fantasy in a Time of Chaos" sprang out of a request from The Living Church (Anglican Communion; where this poem was first published) for poems during the pandemic and some time spent considering the formal elements of Donne's "Song" ("Go and catch a falling star").*

Marly Youmans is the author of fifteen books: her most recent book of poems is *The Book of the Red King* (Montréal: Phoenicia Publishing, 2019); her most recent novel is *Charis in the World of Wonders* (San Francisco: Ignatius Press, 2020).

WE ARE ALL GOD'S POEMS
Jordan Zandi

and we are all God's poems.
There are 17 of us shouldering
a green hill into place
or there are 360 of us shouldering
a green hill into place—
There are more.

The green hill is taking shape.

We'll love the earth then
field-soft and field-bright
and the slopingness of its hill
and the hill like a mountain.

Be here or not here
at what might be the start or the end
of the start of the end
of a return to the original and

◊ *What got me started with this poem was the slippage of uncertainty that exists in the words "we" and "all" (Is we 3? 300?) and how the number can change and the same "we" and "all" would still fit. This suggested to me growth and process—Which also seem akin to and part of the idea of hope.*

Jordan Zandi is the author of *Solarium* (Sarabande Books, 2016), which won the Kathryn A. Morton prize and was named by both the *New Yorker* and the *New York Times* as one of the best poetry books of the year. He holds an M.F.A. in poetry from Boston University, an M.S. in computer science from the University of Chicago and lives in Portland, Oregon, where he works for a data analytics company.

WE ARE ALL GOD'S POEMS
MAYA JEWELL ZELLER

My daughter dreams of digging up lots of dead bodies. A sharp spade; a cut
grub; dull thunk to rock. This is dream now, is hugging our subconscious.

                        A long time ago, I fell asleep on a plastic beach,
                            in a plastic bag,   muttering Moore
    to myself: *If you tell me why the fen*   */ appears impassable, I then* . . .

I say, Digging up bodies? & she says, *Burying* them, Mom, *listen*
for once, they were liquified, filled with red gel & Mom— & I'm back to muttering
Moore— the float of brain

impossible—I then

      Will tell you why I think that I/   *can get across it if I try.*   It was 1909,
                          & things felt more likely, Shackleton
                  crossing a great expanse of ice, searching for god—

My friends were there, my daughter says, to help me, we were all
burying bodies, but it gave us sinus infections. She smiles.

❦

Last week, it was bog bodies. With her, I mean. Bogs, & bodies, & I thought of

            Shackleton, how cold he must have been, believing & not
                believing & saying he believed. I thought of

Borges, revising the Sahara, the sand slipping through fingers,
nearly cliché, & I thought of fourth grade, her mummy phase.

> Wonder: that slow dog, the small one,
> shot for not pulling its weight. I think of how the fur & skin
> must have been preserved in ice, how in peat a carcass stills & appears
> peaceful.

I want to remind her of this, how she sent me articles from *Smithsonian*,
how she showed me the corpses like calcified fish, but

it's time to make breakfast. I pull the veggie patty from its transparent sheath
& think of all the composites I've consumed, so much plastic I probably replaced
the Borges in my Sahara, the salt in my marrow, with microplastic.

> In *Mean Girls*, the villainous crew goes by it:
> The Plastics. I keep thinking of how Regina Jacobs survives the bus.
> It's fiction, but seems just as likely as a bog body, or dog body
> preserved in ice. It's nice, isn't it?

I'm not sure   I am one of God's poems, I think.   I let my daughter
watch this & now she's burying bodies with her friends.   & digging them
up.

Bogs. Bodies & bogs, bogs & —

It was the fault, I think, of my marrow, the pandemic, how bored we all were,
how despairing. *It was funny at the time.*

◊*I'm always interested in myth-making. While writing this poem, I recalled Mary Ruefle saying that Borges claimed to have "rearranged the Sahara" because he picked up and then slowly trailed handfuls of sand. And Paulo Coelho is attributed to telling us how "Borges said there are only four stories. . . a love story between two people, a love story between three people, the struggle for power and the voyage." I was, I think, trying to do all of these--a mother-daughter love story, a mother-daughter-[choose your allusion] love story, plastic and bogs, the Arctic or the desert journey. I wanted to re-hero it, but with girls and dreams and Marianne Moore.*

Maya Jewell Zeller is the author of *Alchemy for Cells & Other Beasts*; *Yesterday, the Bees; & Rust Fish*. She is Associate Professor of English at Central Washington University and Poetry Editor for Scablands Books.

WE ARE ALL G-D'S POEMS
Jana Zvibleman

"Let's see, was it about a parakeet?"

Babbling as I do to help wake us, I tug Bruce's elastic-waist jeans up over his skin-and-bones yet leaden legs. "So, did you have a dream?"

"Yeah . . . but I don't remember it."

His curly-haired head and emaciated torso rise with the bed to an angle. "Let's see," I say, crisscrossing the straps of the Hoyer lift over him. "Was it about . . ." I manage the fasteners. "Was it about a, um, parakeet?"

Where'd that come from? We have nothing to do with parakeets. When I was a girl, I found a green, black, and white one in our backyard, a metal band with numbers on one leg. Tweety Bird lived with us for years, would peck at the cream cheese on a bagel. Bruce's mother, too, once let him have a parakeet. But . . .

He's staring far off. "Yeah. It *was* about a parakeet."
Now he's telling his dream, *yada yada,* parakeet, bench, table . . .

"Bruce! Bruce, this is *something*. You know, it's showing us . . . If you, when . . . when we're not . . . we can still, we'll be able to, um . . . communicate."

After he passed, maybe a century,
I'm sitting at a tiny table in Nancy's P's Cafe, telling this story to a friend. Licking muffin crumbs from my fingertips, I stand, and turn the corner to the back door.
At my eye level, a gold-framed painting: two colorful pastel figures in dapper hats, vests, gloves, monocles, sharing tea. Parakeets.

We cross the street to Bag Ladies, a consignment shop. Now that I've moved on from wearing black only, I rifle through tight racks of blues, greens, reds. A blouse catches my eye: orange, not my color; synthetic, not my fabric;

sleeveless and snug, not my style. Yet, that repeated print of, you know, green birds . . .. I buy it.

◊*My spiritual practice includes trying to be conscious of the presence of G-d. While "chopping wood and carrying water," of course, I often forget. Writing often returns me to the present, so the call to take part in this anthology got my attention.*

Jana Zvibleman, Poet Laureate of her backyard, has collaborated with even a flugelhornist. She appears in journals, including Calyx; anthologies; and chapbooks. Events featuring her include The Magic Barrel. Her play *The Bad Mothers*, premiered in 2017; *Kitty Sews Corsets* in 2018.

WE ARE ALL GOD'S POEMS
Jane Zwart

and among the tells that we are all
God's poems are scores of ghazals
with God's name in the last line.

Among the tells is that we find
our author's name in our throats
even when we do not end our singing

with begging or with praise.

                                        We are all
God's poems and some of us ghazals
and some furious with a God

who could call blame blasphemy
but instead signs our tortured petitions
to recall God. Because God recalls

how we have gouged mountains
and coughed blood, how aimlessness
refuses to slow bullets. God knows

that coffins come in sizes,
that disease and unease do not.

We are all God's poems, and God

does not shirk from the Jeremiad.

Look, we are still kneeling here:

free verse and lamentations.

◊*I tend to believe that poems, like human beings, live & move & have their being somewhere between what their maker intends and what their own will demands. I wanted to write a poem about that daring element of God's providence for us—that room to blame, to challenge God— and thinking about the form of the ghazal—where the writer uses the final line, often, to coil some question or protest back toward self, addressing themselves by name—gave me a way to begin.*

Jane Zwart teaches at Calvin University, where she also directs the Calvin Center for Faith & Writing. Her poems have previously appeared in *Poetry*, *Ploughshares*, and *TriQuarterly*, as well as other journals and magazines.

ABOUT THE EDITORS

SHANN RAY

American Book Award winner Shann Ray teaches leadership and forgiveness studies at Gonzaga University and poetry at Stanford. A National Endowment for the Arts Fellow, through his research in forgiveness and genocide Shann has served as a visiting scholar in Africa, Asia, Europe, and the Americas, and as a poetry mentor for the PEN America Prison and Justice Writers Program. He is the author of *Sweetclover* and *The Souls of Others*.

CINNAMON KILLS FIRST

Cinnamon (Spear) Kills First is a word warrior from the Northern Cheyenne Reservation in Montana. With a Rez education from home, two Ivy League degrees, and an MFA from the Iowa Writers' Workshop, she's a cross-cultural communicator who bridges the gap between Indian Country and the rest of the world.

KEYA MITRA LLOYD

Keya Mitra Lloyd is an associate professor of English at Pacific University. Her fiction has appeared in *The Kenyon Review* (2011 & 2015) and many other publications. Keya has completed two novels, a short-story collection, and a memoir. She lived in India for ten months on a Fulbright grant.

JOSÉ HERNANDEZ

José Hernandez was born and raised in Caracas, Venezuela and has lived in the United States since 1987. He received a Masters of Science and a PhD in Leadership Studies from Gonzaga University. An avid reader of leadership, theology and social issues, José is a quiet activist in conversations over racial injustice and immigration policies related to the developing world. He is the fitness director at Gonzaga University and an independent sports psychology consultant.

PATRICIA VALDÉS

Patricia Valdés spent her childhood in Mexico, she made a home in Spokane where she raised her children, and now delights in her grandchildren, family, friends and community. She served as a therapist in the community, she worked as an administrator and taught at EWU, and currently serves as a bereavement counselor at Hospice of Spokane. She writes poems about social justice.

CHARLES FINN

Charles Finn in the author of *Wild Delicate Seconds: 29 Wildlife Encounters*, *On a Benediction of Wind: Poems a Photographs from the American West*, (winner of the 2022 Montana Book Award) and co-editor of *The Art of Revising Poetry: 21 U.S. Poets on Their Drafts, Craft, and Process*.

ABOUT THE PRESS

Unsolicited Press is based out of Portland, Oregon and focuses on the works of the unsung and underrepresented. As a womxn-owned, all-volunteer small publisher that doesn't worry about profits as much as championing exceptional literature, we have the privilege of partnering with authors skirting the fringes of the lit world. We've worked with emerging and award-winning authors such as Shann Ray, Amy Shimshon-Santo, Brook Bhagat, Kris Amos, and John W. Bateman.

Learn more at unsolicitedpress.com. Find us on twitter and instagram.